ACADIAN HOMECOMING

CONGRÈS MONDIAL ACADIEN

WRITTEN BY CL

PHOTOGRAPHY BY F

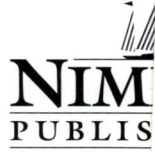

NIM

PUBLIS

This text is from a larger manuscript entitled "Voices of Acadie," by Clive Doucet.

Nimbus Publishing Limited
PO Box 9166
Halifax, NS B3K 5M8
(902) 455-4286

Printed and bound in Canada
Cover Design: Min Landry
Interior Design: Margaret Issenman
Back Cover: Members of the Grand rassemblement jeunesse celebrate their heritage at the closing mass at Grand-Pré, (top).
        Old meets new at the statue of Evangeline at Grand-Pré, (bottom).

Library and Archives Canada Cataloguing in Publication
    Doucet, Clive, 1946-
    Acadian homecoming : the Congrès mondial acadien 2004 / Clive
    Doucet ; photographs by François Gaudet.
    ISBN 1-55109-522-X

1. Congrès mondial acadien (2004 : Nova Scotia) 2. Congrès mondial
acadien (2004 : Nova Scotia)—Pictorial works. 3. Acadians—Interviews.
I. Gaudet, François - II. Title.

FC2045.D68 2005   971.6'004114   C2005-901067-3

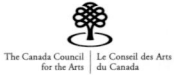

Canadä

We acknowledge the financial support of the Government of Canada through the Book Publishing Industry Development Program (BPIDP) and the Canada Council, and of the Province of Nova Scotia through the Department of Tourism, Culture and Heritage for our publishing activities.

ACKNOWLEDGMENTS

I would like to thank all those who so kindly agreed to talk to me during the Congrès mondial acadien 2004. The Congrès was a beehive of activity from one end of Nova Scotia to the other, and often even a few minutes for an unplanned interview weren't easy to find. There were great musicians to be heard, programs to attend, relatives to visit, art to see, and delicious meals to be consumed. For sixteen days, the Grand-Pré National Historic Site became a formal and informal university of Acadie, with authors, musicians, artists, dancers, and academics from every corner of Acadie coming to visit, talk, sing, learn, and teach. However, people still took the time to share their stories.

Donna Doucet, director of the Société promotion Grand-Pré, found time to sit with me on a bench in the interpretation centre and talk about her own Acadian journey. I interrupted Jonathan Fowler, the archeologist at Grand-Pré, as he was wrapping up the last few days of his summer dig, but he took the time to walk me around the site, explaining carefully the results of his work. Paul Comeau, chef and owner of Chez Christophe, which was packed from morning to night, came in early one day to talk about his restaurant and food. Edna Chiasson in Chéticamp was besieged by visitors at the Artisanat (the artisan's workshop) wanting explanations of the old *métiers*, but she took time during lunch to talk with me. I managed to have a conversation with Barbara Leblanc on the very day she launched "Tous ensemble," Nova Scotia's new traditional dance program for school children. Douglas Lapierre of Chezzetcook and I talked on the steps of the Metro Centre in Halifax, just after we had met in the line-up to buy our tickets for the final concert.

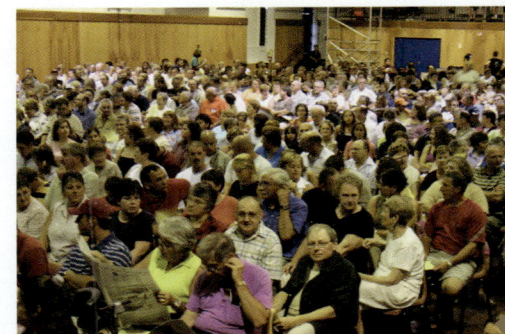

A packed house in Chéticamp. Spectators waiting for the Grand Cercle performance to begin are in for a visual and cultural delight.

And so it went: a scramble of impromptu moments over sixteen days that together add up to Acadian Homecoming and the Congrès mondial acadien 2004. And in spite of the often-rushed circumstances, I was always impressed with participants' thoughtful eloquence. I have done my best to transcribe the interviews exactly as they were given. No doubt there are some imperfections, both in my hurried notes and in my translations, but I trust the words come across as people meant them, and that you will be as charmed and enlightened as I was by the voices of Acadie.

The beautiful photographs of François Gaudet speak for themselves.

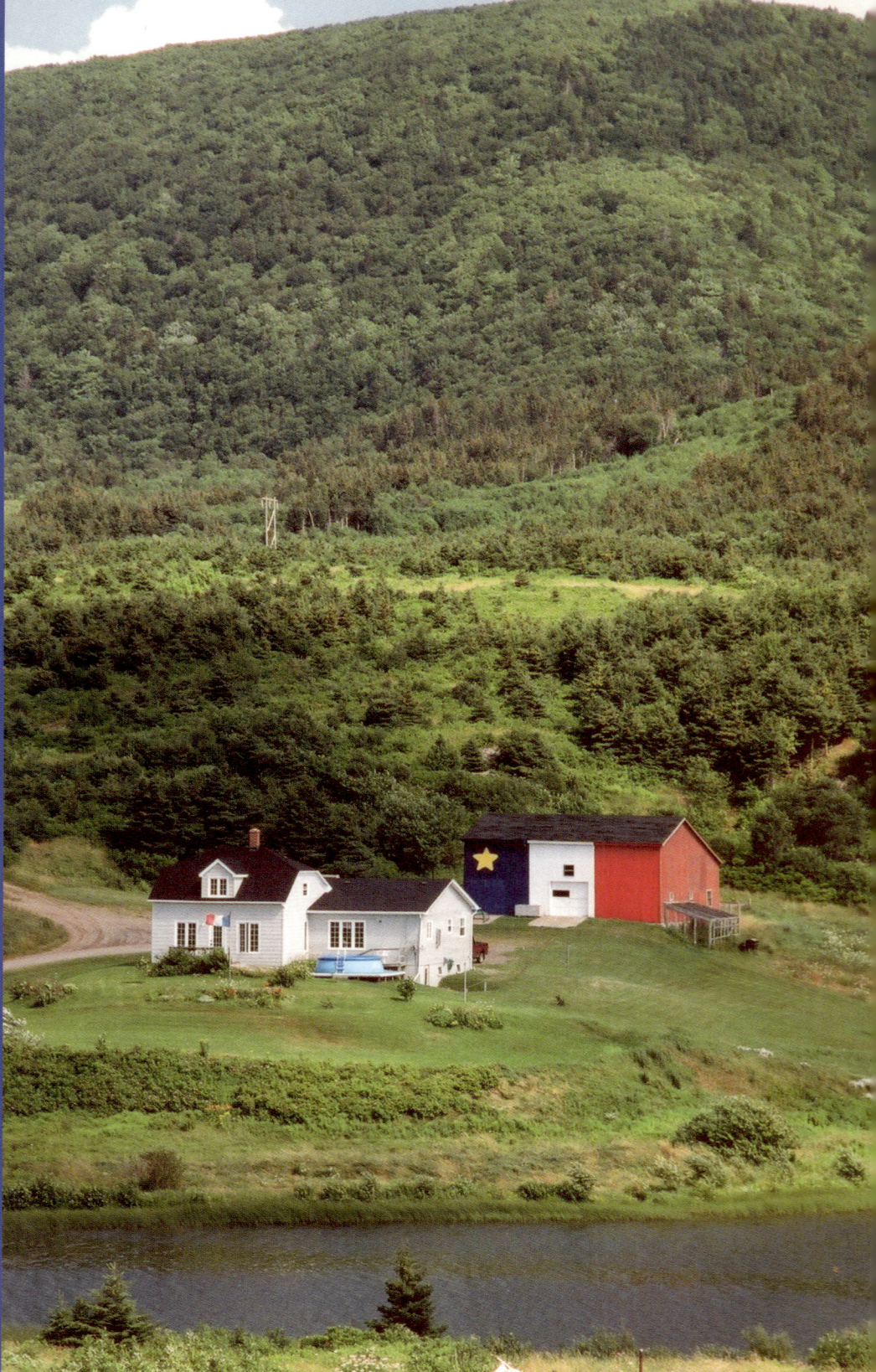

A barn dressed in Acadian colours, Grand Étang.

Contents

INTRODUCTION   1

1   OPENING DAYS, CHURCH POINT, BAIE STE.-MARIE   5
Conversations with Paul Foster (Amirault), Donald J. Arceneaux, Paul Caissie
and Jeanne Doucet, Paul Comeau, Amanda Lafleur

2   GENEALOGY   14
Conversations with Marielle Bourgeois, Stephen White, Burke Macdonnell
and Georgette Burke

3   EVANGELINE, GRAND-PRÉ, AND THE NATIONAL HISTORIC SITE   19
Conversations with Norman Godin, Jonathan Fowler, Donna Doucet

4   FATHER ANSELME CHIASSON AND FATHER DANIEL BOUDREAU   28

5   LE MI-TEMPS, CHÉTICAMP   31
Conversations with Edna Chiasson, Maurice Poirier, John Macdonald, Barbara Leblanc

6   MUSICIANS, WRITERS, AND VISUAL ARTISTS   38
Conversations with Denise Comeau, William Roach, Elizabeth Lefort, Michel Williatte-Battet

7   YOUTH ASSEMBLY AND WOMEN'S SUMMIT   48
Conversations with Stephanie Gaudet, Guy Gallant, Remi Leger, Veronique
and Catherine Kinney, Laurette Deveau, Ruth Blanchard, Cynthia Holland, Elaine Clement

8   Acadian Schools   54
Conversations with Fernand Doucet, Sally Ross, Douglas LaPierre, Allister Surette

9   Closing Mass, Grand-Pré   60
Conversation with Cyprien Okana

10   Closing Concert, Citadel Hill   66
Conversations with Douglas LaPierre, Pat Gionet (Carrière), Delphine Gionet Bergeron,
Jeanne Gionet, and Monsieur Surette

11   Highlights from the Family Reunions   74
Gaudet, Amirault, Mius/Muise/Meuse, Doucet

Conclusion   79

Family Reunion Organizers   82

No one really knows precisely what the Congrès mondial acadien is; it means different things to different people. For many, it's a time to attend a giant family reunion and see cousins they haven't seen since school days and cousins they never even knew they had. For others, it's an opportunity to study genealogy and family history, or to give a paper at an academic conference. For musicians it's the chance to play before thousands of appreciative fans. For artists and authors it's the chance to sell paintings and books, and for everybody it's the chance to express a fierce and enduring pride in one's Acadian identity.

During the Congrès mondial acadien 2004, a thousand events and a hundred family reunions were spread from the villages of Argyle and Pubnico at the southern edge of Nova Scotia to Chéticamp and Grand Étang near the tip of Cape Breton Island. A ten-hour drive separates these two Acadian regions. The Acadian communities of Nova Scotia are flung like dots across a broad map. After the Seven Years' War, when the Acadians began to trickle back from Europe, the hills of Madawaska, and the American seaboard, they were not allowed to return to their former villages around the Bay of Fundy, places like Grand-Pré, Minas, and Beaubassin. Nor were they allowed to settle in contiguous settlements so that their communities might again become the political force they had been. This is the reason that today, 250 years later, the Acadian communities of Nova Scotia remain isolated.

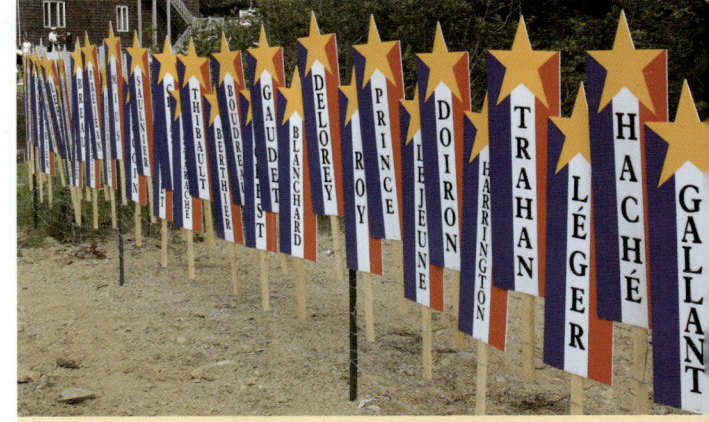

Acadian family names stand on proud display at Church Point. Though certain names, such as "Leblanc" and "Surette," are immediately recognizable, up to three hundred Acadian family names can be traced to pre-expulsion Acadia, from church and government documents.

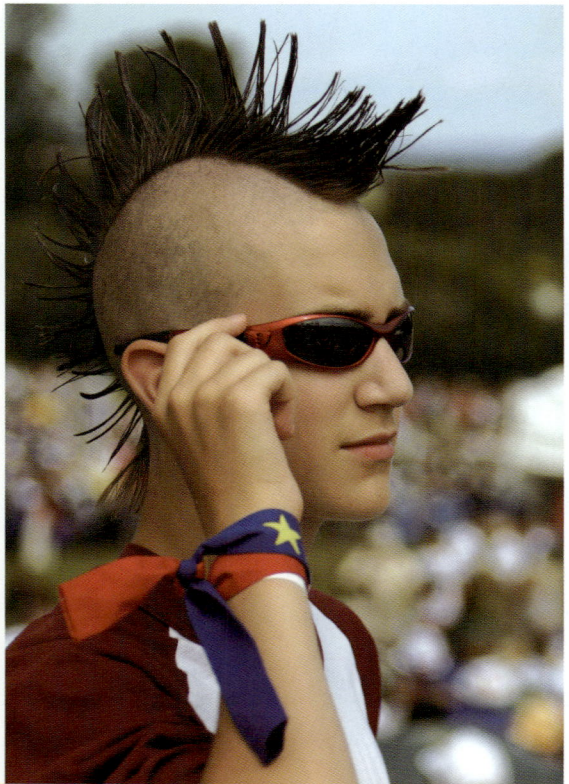 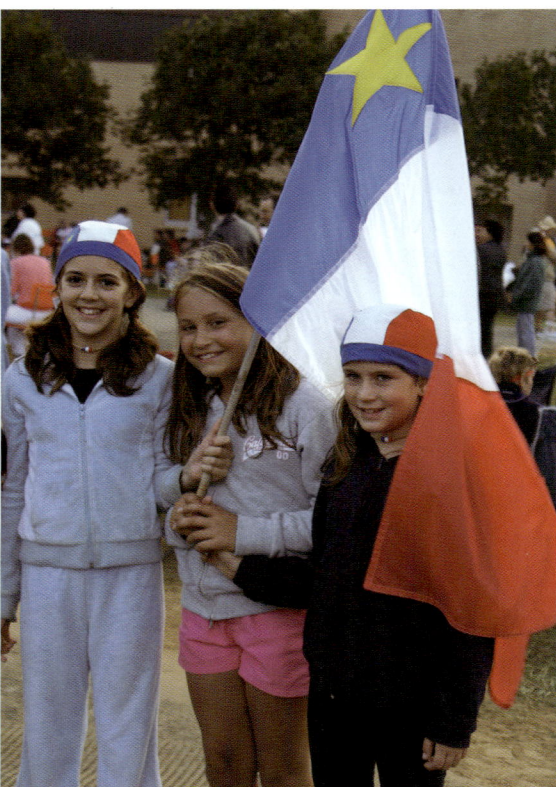

L: A young Acadian has a chance to look to the past and think about the future during the spectacular religious and musical event at the Grand-Pré National Historic Site.

R: Young participants Jessica Wilson, Danielle Gaudet, and Vanessa Wilson proudly show off their Acadian colours.

Prior to the Congrès, I had never visited the villages of Baie Ste.-Marie. My sense of Acadie was rooted in my family and the village of Grand Étang. In this way of thinking, I am not alone. But for me and other Acadians, the Congrès is the great exception, the time when it is possible to visit many places and talk with Acadians from all over the world—from Louisiana, Europe, and all over Maritime Canada. For sixteen days, a complex and wonderful city arises as if from the very air, and in that magical place gather citizens of the world—children, parents, elders, dancers, musicians, singers, artists, scientists, politicians, chefs, journalists, poets, teachers, fishermen, farmers, Métis and Mi'kmaq. The thing that binds them together is that they all call themselves Acadians and together they form Acadie.

Acadie is unusual, because it has no political boundaries, no army, no customs officers, no border crossings. You have to discover Acadie by and for yourself. But it is real, and you always know when you are in it. Acadie could be in a Louisiana parish hall on a burning hot August afternoon; the Acadian peninsula in New Brunswick on a chill October morning; a busy pub in Ottawa. But for sixteen days, the Congrès mondial acadien becomes the temporary capital of Acadie. For sixteen days, Acadians from all over the world gather to talk, drink, eat, and celebrate being Acadian.

There have been Acadian assemblies before. The best known were the ones of 1881 and 1884, when the Acadian flag and national anthem were chosen. These assemblies represented the first public acknowledgement of Acadian survival in Canada, and the first reconnection of Acadians as a people. But until 1994, no one had ever tried to assemble the Acadians from the many different places they had been sent to in 1755. Nor did many think that such an assembly was possible. But some Acadians from Alberta decided it could be done, and, led by André Boudreau, they organized a world gathering.

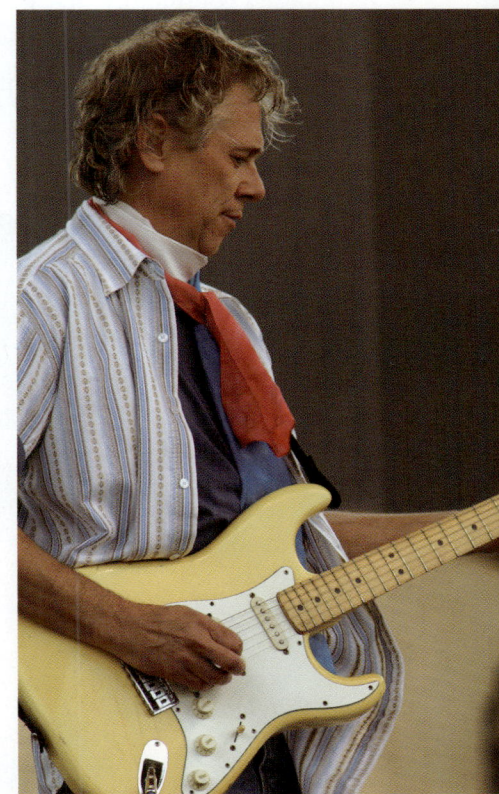

Pierre Robichaud from the acclaimed group 1755 performs with an Acadian scarf around his neck, a symbol of his proud ancestry.

In 1994, to everyone's astonishment, a quarter of a million Acadians answered the call and came to New Brunswick. The United Nations labeled it the cultural event of the century. And five years later, the second world gathering was held in Louisiana. This was a different kind of miracle. For northern Acadians, Louisiana has mythical qualities. Many of our ancestors settled there, but it's so different from the north, with its tropical heat and bayous, that it seems more a dream than reality. There for the first time, we met our long-lost cousins and had a chance to see the kind of homes and villages they had built for themselves in the Mississippi delta. The discovery was wonderful.

The third Congrès was held in 2004 in Nova Scotia, the birthplace of Acadie and the place where, four hundred years ago, our ancestors built the dykes that created thousands of acres of rich farmland. In Nova Scotia they had created a unique society: the first of the New World settlements to reject feudalism, the first to have an independent political voice that was neither British or French, the first to have a name that was neither New France nor New England, but truly new: Acadie. Nova Scotian Acadians were the first to have a partnership, and not a war, with the native people. The memory of the place, after its destruction, had such echoes of utopia that a hundred years later it inspired a great American poet to compose a poem that would be read by millions and endure across centuries.

In 2004, over two hundred thousand people came to Nova Scotia for the Congrès mondial acadien to see where Acadie began. The next Congrès will be in 2009, in the Acadian Peninsula of New Brunswick. It will have its own flavour, but the Nova Scotia Congrès represents the completion of a cycle. It marked the four hundredth anniversary of the arrival of the first French-speaking settlers, and was the third and final stop in the trilogy of reunions that has begun to reconnect a community that was broken and scattered 250 years ago.

Here are some photographs and stories from that vast celebration. We hope they capture some of the excitement, the hopes, and the joie de vivre of the Acadian people. There will not be another celebration like it.

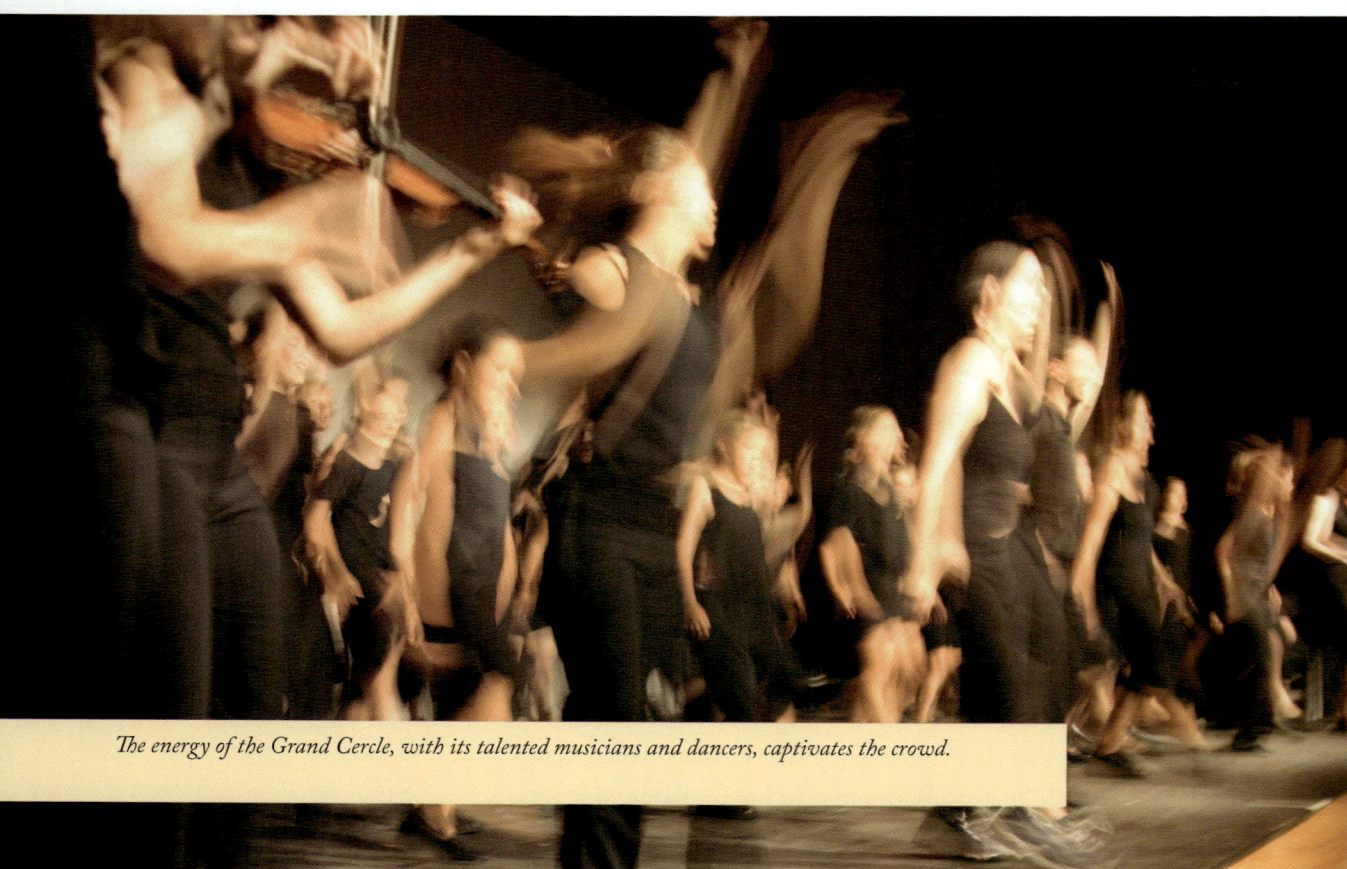

The energy of the Grand Cercle, with its talented musicians and dancers, captivates the crowd.

1

OPENING DAYS, CHURCH POINT, BAIE STE.-MARIE

Longfellow's Evangeline never made it back to her native Acadie, but many fellow Acadians did. Some of them actually walked back from New England to the Annapolis Valley, but it had been taken over by British settlers. Eventually, a number of Acadians were able to move on and settle along St. Mary's Bay (Baie Ste.-Marie). On this windswept and rocky coastline, the sea provided their livelihood while the forests provided wood for seaworthy fishing boats. Today's Acadians have developed this coastline into a gem worthy to be discovered and experienced.

– from Baie Ste.-Marie travel brochure,
 published by the Municipality of Clare

The Congrès opened with a mass in the great wooden church at Church Point, the largest wooden church in North America. The building is so imposing it seems to anchor the village physically. The outside may be sombre, but the interior is a brilliant kaleidoscope of colours, paintings, and statues. As the mass began, Acadians were still pouring into the little villages strung for forty kilometres along the narrow Baie Ste.-Marie, which is created by the great spit of land jutting down from the town of Digby and Annapolis Royal (once Port-Royal).

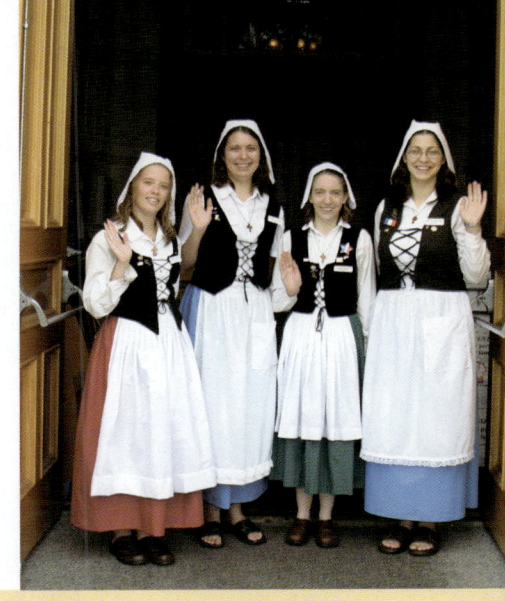

A friendly Acadian bonjour and welcome from the guides at Sainte-Marie Church. Sainte-Marie, the largest wooden church in North America, was built between 1903 and 1905 with the help of 1,500 local volunteers. From left to right, Rachel Gauvin, Clarice Valontair, Lyanne Comeau, and Lisette Valotaire are all smiles.

Ten of the hundred family reunions happened in the villages of Baie Ste.-Marie: the Beliveaus, Doucets, Gaudets, Comeaus, Dugases, Leblancs, Maillets, Robichauds, Saulniers, and Theriaults. At the Université Sainte-Anne at Church Point, there was also an academic conference with more than a hundred speakers from Canada, Louisiana and France, and a musical adaptation of *Evangeline*. In Halifax, there was a women's summit and a youth assembly. And these were just the larger events: each village had its own galaxy of celebrations, from opera star Suzy Leblanc's concert at the great church of St. Bernard to Le grand cercle, an original musical performed by students in Chéticamp with members of the Nova Scotia orchestra. In Chéticamp, the population tripled for the Congrès. There were over 7,000 visitors in a village of only 3,500 people. Every house, hotel, motel, and campsite was full, and there were more events than there was time to attend them.

At the Suzy Leblanc concert, I met some acquaintances from Ottawa. They were Franco-Ontarians, and I asked them what brought them so far from home. They replied, "We just like the cultural liveliness of Acadians. What better place to spend our holidays?"

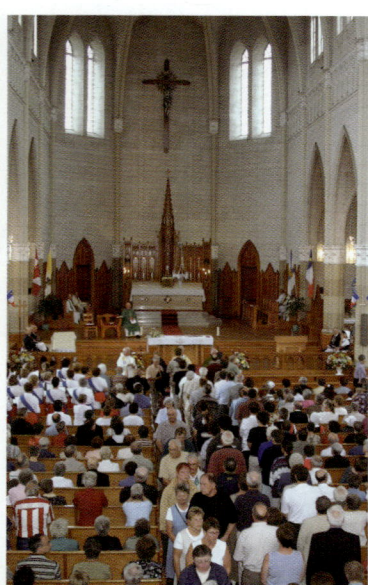
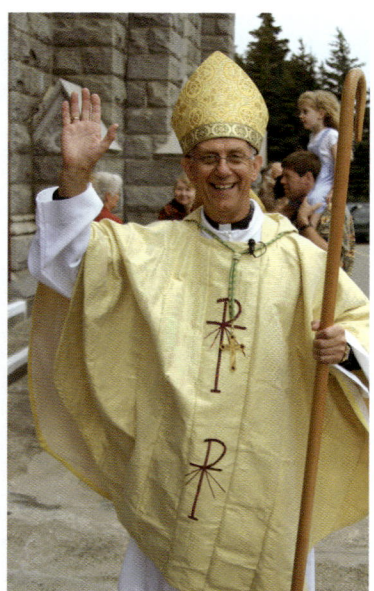

The traditional sounds of opening mass ring through Saint-Bernard Church in the municipality of Clare. This impressive stone church, due to its wonderful acoustics, hosts an internationally-acclaimed, classical music festival every year.

Monseigneur André Richard ensures that all visiting Acadians seeking to honour their traditional Roman Catholic roots will feel welcome.

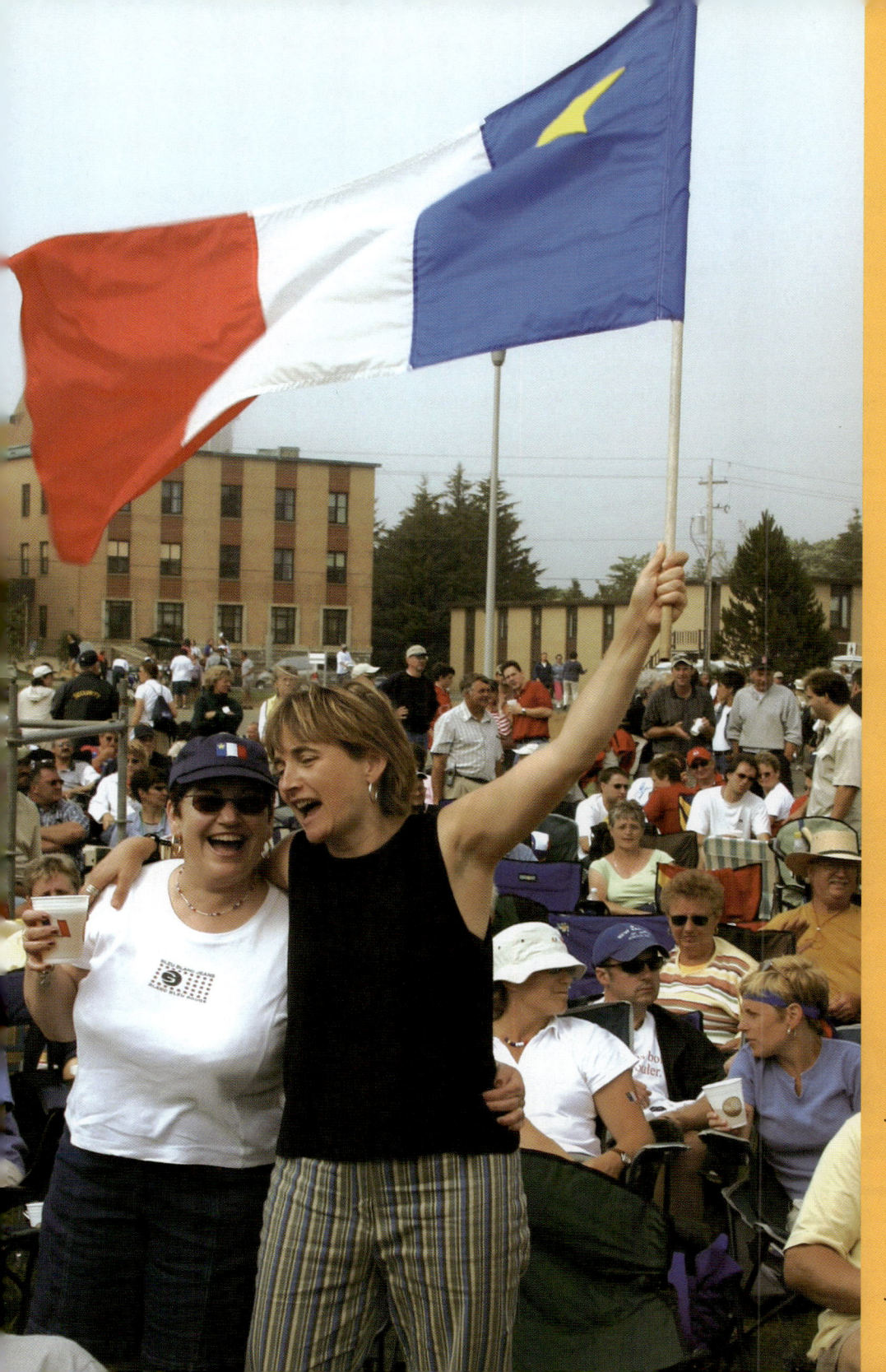

The opening ceremonies at Church Point swarm with excited Acadians eager to start off events. Denise Comeau and Joanne Landry sing along with band 1755's eclectic "Acadian style" folk rock at the opening ceremonies on July 31.

PAUL FOSTER (AMIRAULT), TORONTO

I came as a response to a Quebecois friend, who dared me to come and explore my Acadian roots. I've used the Congrès as a jumping-off point to explore the region and its history, to hear what other people think Acadians are, and to ponder what an Acadian is for me.

DONALD J. ARCENEAUX, LOUISIANA AND IOWA

I grew up in Louisiana and still go back for two months every year. In Iowa, I'm a forestry data collection technician. I never heard about the first Congrès in New Brunswick but I sure did the second. In Louisiana, I helped out with four family reunions because my grandparents are divided between four families: Arceneaux, Boudreau, Préjean, and Broussard. They are all big Acadian families, especially the Arceneaux. I think all the Préjeans ended up in Louisiana because I've never met or heard of a Préjean here.

My father was an agricultural banker and my mother was a teacher and a librarian. Both grew up very poor. Grandfather was a sharecropper and Dad grew up a farm boy. My mother's father passed away when she was two, and my grandmother, a true Broussard, raised all four kids by herself.

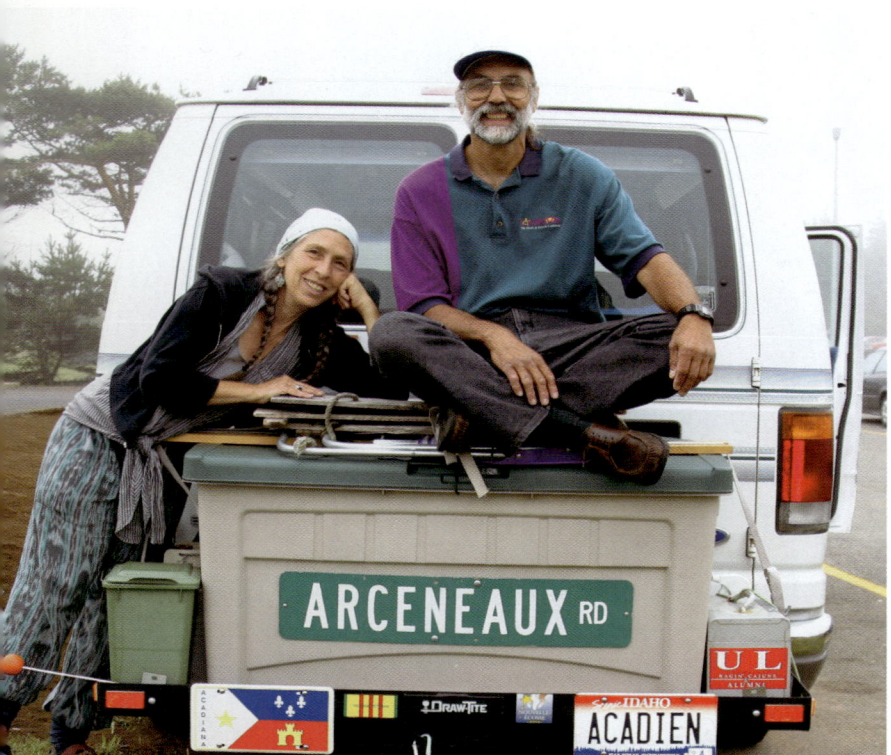

The Congrès definitely evoked the spirit of pilgrimage, as many Acadians travelled far and wide to join the festivities. Donald Joseph Arceneaux and Kent Miriam travelled from far the southern US, but a few miles could not keep Donald from making merry with his Acadian cousins in Nova Scotia.

I went through half my life as a teen and a young person knowing I was Acadian but not really connecting with its significance. The Cajun Renaissance in Louisana began in the 1970s just as I was leaving home. I grew up with *boudin* and *fais do-dos* and the sound of French. It was part of my life, but I never gave it much thought until I left Louisiana and began to reflect on all that I had been part of when I was young.

For me the Congrès is a celebration of family and our history. It's exciting for me because it's the first time I've ever visited where we came from. I'm here to discover the natural environment, the landscape, the culture; to meet cousins; to tell stories—the whole shot. I want to see the Acadian willow trees at Grand-Pré and I want to see where the apple orchards grew. The MacIntosh apple was created by crossing a French tree with a native one. I've heard about the Acadian orchards of Grand-Pré, about how when a young couple was married, the first thing the woman did was plant the orchard; that was her domain. And from willow bark, of course, comes

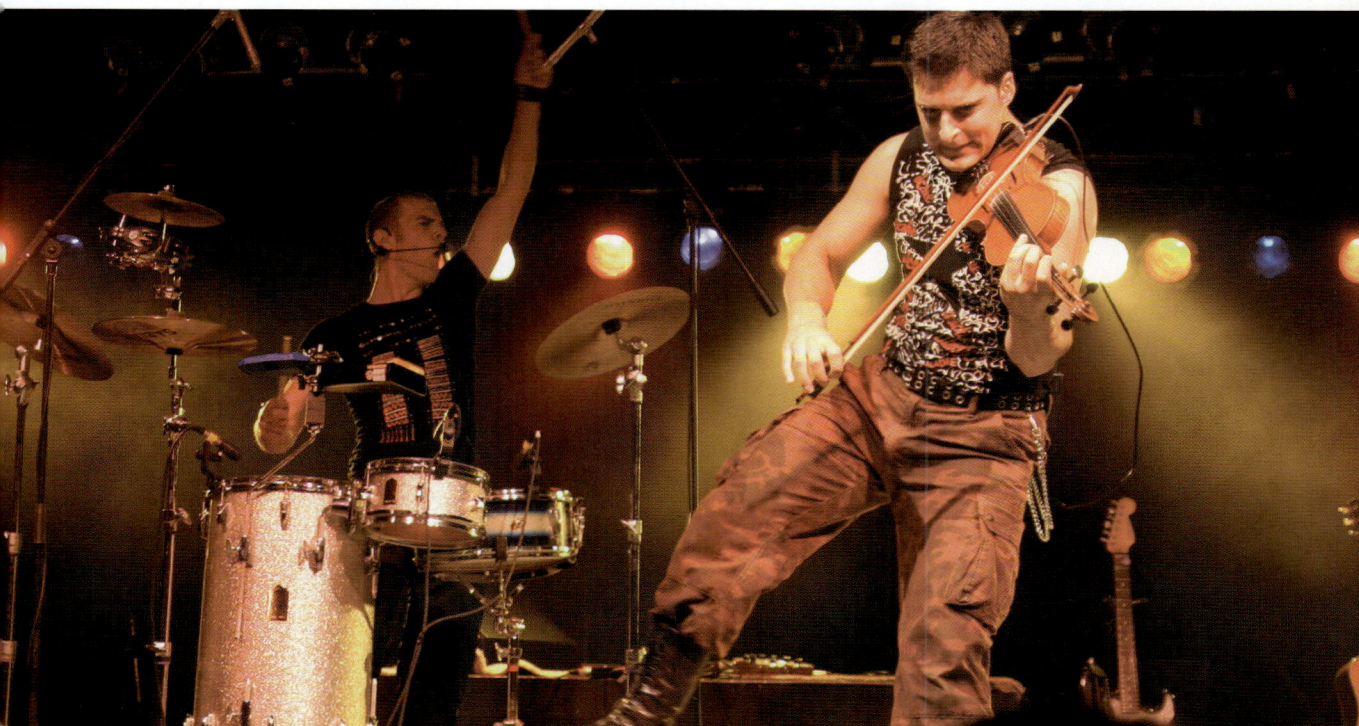

Brian Melanson and Daniel Leblanc from the Acadian band Grand Dérangement give a spectacular performance at the Cape Breton Arena in Chéticamp. Grand Dérangement's eclectic fusion of traditional Acadian music with Celtic and rock has world-wide appeal.

acetylsalicylic acid—aspirin. I'm not sure if we learned that from the Mi'kmaq or they learned it from us. One thing's for sure, neither of us made any money off it.

Our ancestors were deported not by the people who are here, but by governments. I didn't come here to show a fist to those who are here. If someone had offered Acadians free, beautiful land, I'm sure Cajuns would have jumped at it also. I've come here to celebrate the lives of my ancestors; their survival made my life possible. One of my prayers is that they're looking down on me and they're smiling. I think they know it's okay to be different.

Oh, one more thing. It's important. I don't think the Congrès is about the past. It's about the future. All the connections that will be made here—the social, the cultural, the political, the economic, the spiritual—they are all needed for Acadie to continue.

The Blomidon Lookoff between Wolfville and Cape Blomidon provides an incredible view of the Annapolis Valley and the Minas Basin. Many travellers stopped to take in the glorious view of this traditional Acadian land on their way to the celebrations at nearby Grand-Pré.

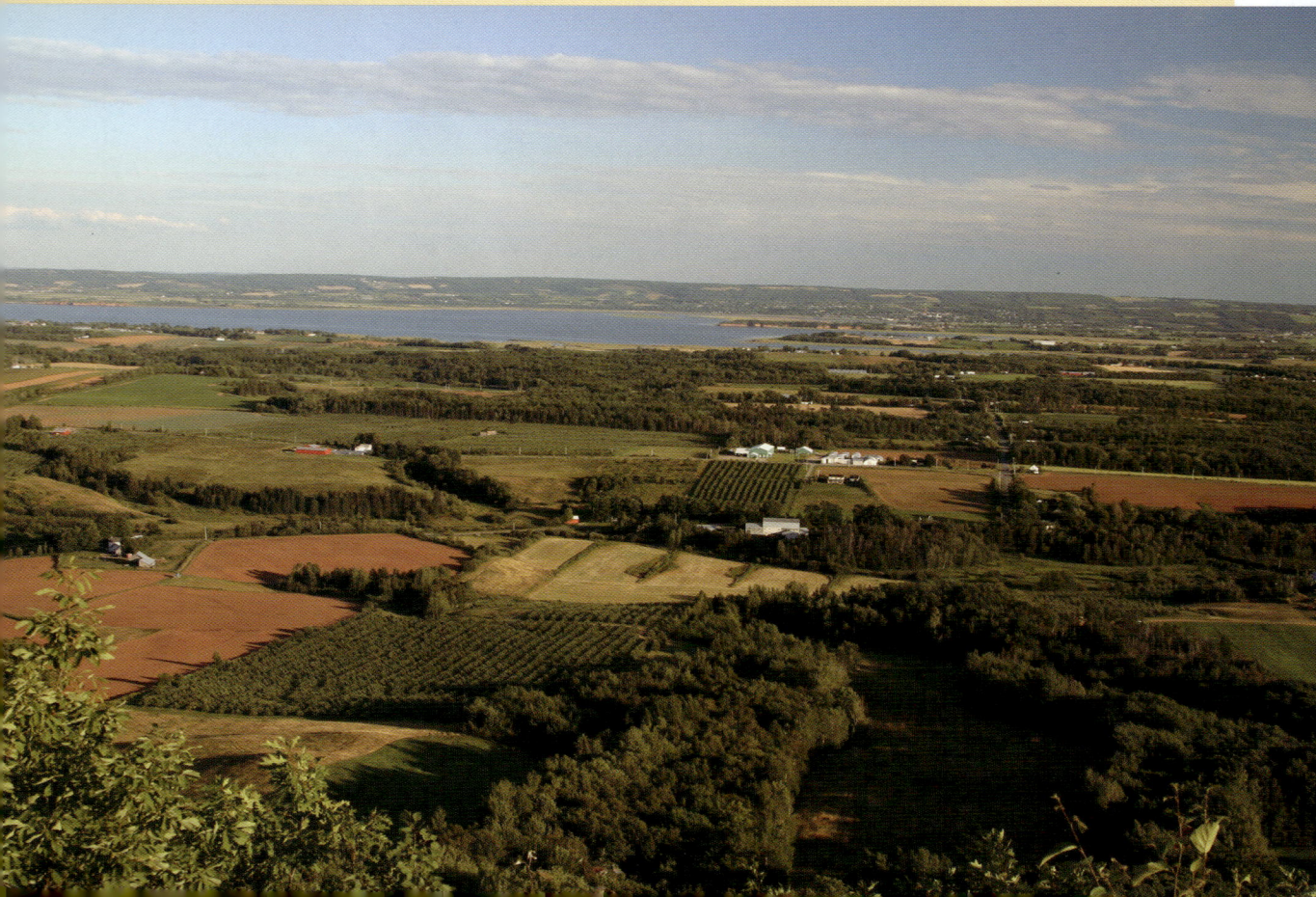

PAUL CAISSIE AND JEANNE DOUCET, SEDGEWICK, MAINE

Jeanne: I was born and brought up in Moncton. Paul was born and brought up in Waltham and then moved to Belmont, near Waltham. Our families knew each other. We first met when we were two years old in an aunt's house. When we got married, we moved to Marlborough, Massachusetts. There was a French church there; that was the reason we moved there. We wanted to be married in French. I raised four children: three boys and a girl. We've retired to a place called Sedgewick, which is named after Colonel Robert Sedgewick, who defeated our ancestor Captain Germain Doucet at Fort Pentagoet. We get great delight in flying the Acadian flag at our front door in Sedgewick.

Paul: I worked as an engineer for many years and then went into vocational training. Then Jeanne did too.

Jeanne: We both wanted our children to speak French, and spoke only French in the house when our first son was young.

Paul: I didn't know a word of English when my parents sent me to school and I survived. I thought my kids would too.

Jeanne: But our son was slow to start speaking. We thought speaking French in the house was delaying his speech. So we decided to stop speaking French.

Paul: It took quite some time to identify that our children had dyslexia and this was the reason they had trouble putting symbols and sounds together. They have all done well, but they had to work very hard and so did we.

Jeanne: We formed an Acadian cultural society called Le Reveil Acadien. It has eight hundred members worldwide and a quarterly newsletter that runs about thirty pages.

Paul: I don't think many Acadians in Canada know much about the history of Acadie in New England. There is a film called *Waking up French* by Ben Levine that I always tell people to see if they want to get started.

Jeanne: *Waking up French* is about some Acadian kids who go off to university. Some of them speak a few words of French but most of them don't, and then at university, they suddenly hear some of the stories of their parents' and grandparents' lives. It's a history that they never realized was there because their parents wanted to make it easier for them by "blending in." So they spoke English at home and "blended."

Paul: How many people know the Ku Klux Klan was very active in Maine and persecuted anyone who was seen as "ethnic"?

Jeanne: In Ellsworth, a village between Bangor and Bar Harbour, the Klan burned the Acadian church down to the ground twice. *Waking up French* is about waking up to who your parents and grandparents have been. They don't renounce their sense of being American, but their sense of themselves changes.

Paul: My grandmother Caissie lived in Waltham for seventy years. She never learned any English. I think in the back of her mind, she always intended to go back to Canada, but when you have ten kids and put down roots, going back isn't so easy.

Jeanne: We found that with the Le Reveil acadien newsletter, there was this great thirst for knowledge. People loved the stories, the history, the music, the recipes; that's why it's been so successful for twenty years. And now some younger people are coming forward to take over, which is good. The co-editors of the newsletter are now Doris Leger, who is the sister of Viola Leger, the actor who plays La Sagouine, and Paul's cousin, Judy Aucoin.

Paul: At the Fitchburgh Public Library, we now have a whole room dedicated to Acadie.

Jeanne: We have been to all three Congrès mondials and if we're on the earth for the fourth, we will go to it also.

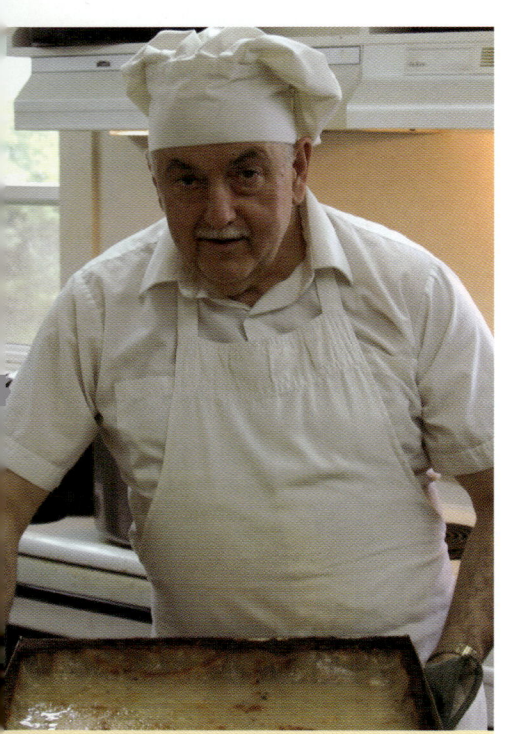

Chef Paul Comeau of Chez Christophe inspects a large Rappie pie, a hearty meat and potato dish traditional to Acadian cuisine, before sliding it back in the oven to get golden brown just in time for supper and the kitchen party.

PAUL COMEAU, PRINCIPAL CHEF AND FOUNDER OF CHEZ CHRISTOPHE, GROSSE COCQUES, BAIE STE.-MARIE

My mother was born in Grosse Cocques in this house, but my career as a chef was a late-blooming vocation. I didn't start until I was forty-five. Prior to that I worked at various jobs for the Association of Fishermen. I cooked for the family and as a volunteer at community events, where I specialized in the traditional Acadian cuisine. It's a simple cuisine, le rapure, le fricôt. It's very different from the Louisiana cooking, which is spicy. I admire the Louisiana chefs. They are animated. They are artists and that shows itself in their food. You have to cook with conviction and passion for it to mean anything, and the Louisiana chefs do. Here in the north, we like our food bland. One of the problems with food that is not spiced is that the line between what is delicious and what is ordinary is narrow. There's not much room for error. When I first opened up my restaurant, very few people had much confidence that the village needed another restaurant. "Fancy food! Who needs that?" I couldn't even get a line of credit from the bank. The funny thing is now my greatest supporters are people from the community; that's been my greatest success.

I have tried lots of new things since I opened up, as well as the traditional dishes like râpure and fricadelles (fish cakes). All the recipes have been successful.

We are opening up a guest house also this summer, right across the street, and I am slowly bringing younger people into the restaurant to train them. I'm not a fan of the kinds of training I see youngsters get in the schools. They train kids to fry things and be good cafeteria cooks. I have a young man who couldn't do well at school at all. Other kids made fun of him. He came from difficult family circumstances. He's doing just fine here.

Moving cooking from the family kitchen into creating a distinctive cuisine that is respected around the world is the great accomplishment of the Louisiana chefs. We can do the same here, but it's going to take a different kind of imagination in the kitchen because our ingredients and kitchen traditions are different.

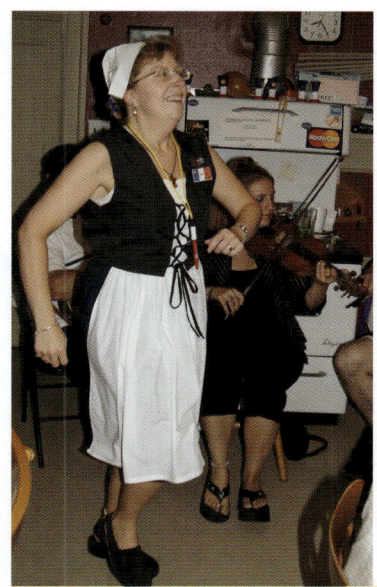

The infectious music of the kitchen party prompts a server to take a minute between guests to do a little two-step at Chez Christophe's.

AMANDA LAFLEUR, FRENCH PROFESSOR, LAFAYETTE, LOUISIANA

I grew up in Evangeline Parish in the north of Louisiana. It is a French area of Louisiana, but not all Acadian. There were different waves of French settlers. The earliest were the men who came down the Mississippi River with LaSalle and never went home. There was a wave of soldiers who came after the fall of Napoleon in Europe. They were mercenaries who had no place to go in Europe after Napoleon was defeated. Then there are the Acadians exiled from Canada, but they didn't come to Louisiana directly. They spent thirty years in France before they left again to come back to the New World. I'm guessing they probably thought they were coming back to a place like Grand-Pré. Louisana is a little different.

Today I live in Lafayette, where I teach Cajun French at the university of Southern Louisiana. My husband teaches logic. I have two sons and they go to school in French. My husband has learned to speak French also. My sons are petits Louisiannais; they like sports and fishing. Their friends get a kick out of it when they hear French in our house. I'm here for the academic conference to talk about standard French and Cajun French.

2

GENEALOGY

It is through learning the names of our ancestors that we have revived Acadie and assured the continuity of our people, but you have to know the names. The names give feelings and meanings. The names allow our ancestors to talk with us.

– Marielle Bourgeois

The heart of the Congrès mondial was family reunions—good food, good music, and the study of genealogy. Every family reunion had several genealogists present. The Doucet family reunion had three: Patricia Doucet Hayes, president of "Les Doucet du Monde," the Doucet family's genealogical society; Stephen White, from the Centre for Acadian Studies; and Marielle Bourgeois. Stephen spoke at the reunion, and then answered questions. These question-and-answer sessions are always intense. During the Doucet family reunion, one woman stood up to say that she had traced all of her family lines back to 1632 and Germain Doucet, but there was one line that eluded her. She had come up against a brick wall when she got to this name and wondered if Stephen could help her. Then she gave the name. Stephen White looked down at his papers, but before he could reply, a man jumped up from the opposite end of the gymnasium and called in a strong, excited voice, "I'm here! I'm from that line!"

This kind of experience was repeated in all family reunions, and the jigsaw puzzles of family histories have been slowly pieced together.

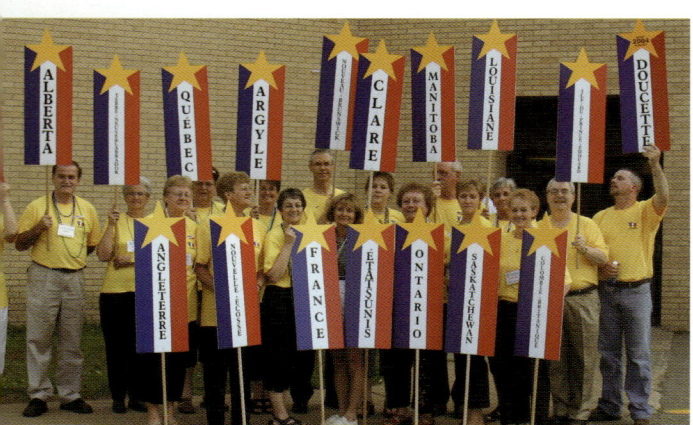

The Doucet participants of the parade of provinces, states, and countries proudly hold their signs high. Due to the scattering of their population after expulsion, Acadians can be found in the far reaches of the globe.

CONVERSATION WITH MARIELLE BOURGEOIS, CALIFORNIA

Marielle: I have lived in California for twenty-two years, but my Acadian adventure began at school in Quebec. For some reason—perhaps it was a school project, I can't remember now—I got interested in genealogy. I traced my family's history in Quebec without too much difficulty, but there was one branch of the family I couldn't find at all, and I contacted a professional genealogist. As soon as he saw the name, he said, "You will have to look outside Quebec." That's when I discovered the Acadian story.

My ancestors were Acadians. Reading about them was like walking through a door and discovering a whole new world that you never imagined existed. My ancestors were at Grand-Pré when the men were locked in the church. The women were loaded onto ships, then the men onto other ships. There is hardly an Acadian family that didn't wonder where a brother or sister went and what happened to them.

Clive: My family was deported from Beaubassin. They were all shipped to France, and then the ones that survived ended up in Louisiana. I have a lot of relatives in Louisiana who look just like my Canadian uncles and aunts. But for some reason, Jean-Marie Doucet escaped into the woods. He was only eight years old.

Marielle: I think I can tell you why. They locked the men up in the church, ten years old and above. Eight years would have been too young.

Clive: Are you sure?

Marielle: That's what happened in Grand-Pré. I'm guessing it was the same at Beaubassin but to be sure, you would have to check John Winslow's diary. It's all written there. The Acadians were the first victims of international conflict to arrive in American ports. With the exception of Philadelphia, where Quakers helped them, they weren't welcome. Many ships were obliged to set sail again, this time for

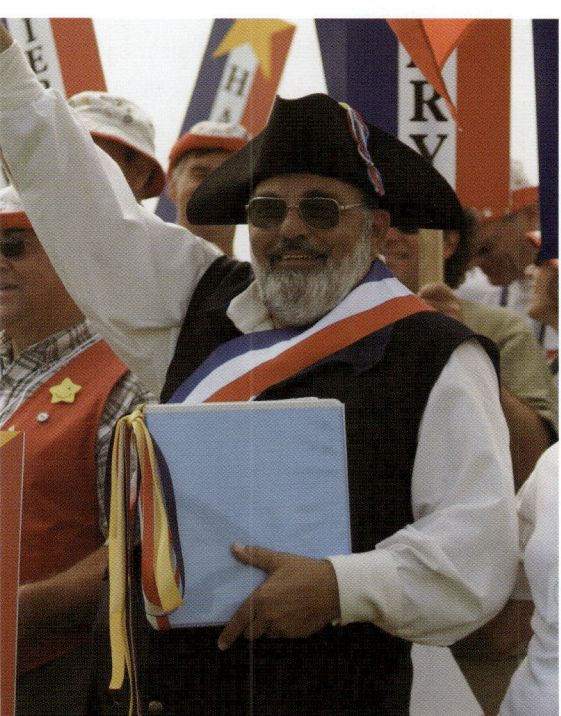

Jean Gaudet celebrates after his voyage Acadie –Fierté, which ended at the memorial church at Grand-Pré. Such events keep the vital Acadian history alive.

Europe, usually with inadequate supplies. Many died on the ships, which became jails in foreign harbours. They died of diseases. All the diseases they had been free of in Acadie—smallpox, cholera, typhus—swept through the places where they were interned. Entire families were extinguished. Some names never reappear again. For those who did survive, one third ended up in Louisiana, one third went to Quebec, one third were scattered. I read all this history as a school girl and it made an enormous impression on me. It was like discovering a world that had always been there, surrounding me, that I'd just never seen before.

I realized that in my class, I was surrounded by descendants of the deportation—Petit Pas, Boudreau, Pellerin, Poirier, Dugas, Arseneault, Cormier, Doucet—all those family names. My best friend was Evangeline Gaudreau. When I told the story to my classmates, they were all astonished. None of them had any idea that their ancestors had lived in any place but Quebec. They thought that they had just gotten straight off the boat from France. It was as if the history of Acadie had been rubbed out with an eraser.

Genealogical research has taken me all over the world. It is one of the great passions of my life.

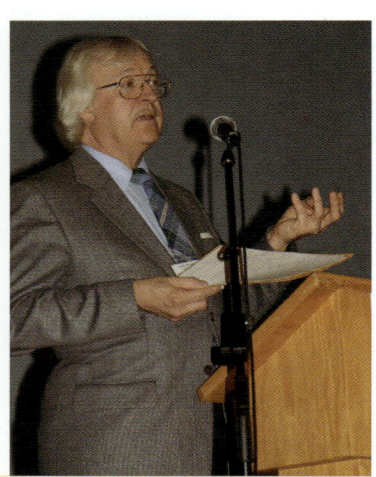

Stephen White lectures on Acadian geneaology. The authority on Acadian genealogy, Stephen has been a genealogist the Centre of Acadian Study at Moncton University for twenty years. He is currently in the midst of working on Dictionnaire généalogique des familles acadiennes, a fully comprehensive database.

When you know the names of your ancestors, I am sure that you can communicate with them. I feel the presence of my Bourgeois ancestors here in this village when I walk in the cemetery. I have become very good friends with Monsieur George Bourgeois of Baton Rouge. We have the same ascendants.

It is through learning the names of our ancestors that we have revived Acadie and assured the continuity of our people, but you have to know the names. The names give feelings and meanings. The names allow our ancestors to talk with us.

CONVERSATION WITH STEPHEN WHITE, GENEALOGIST, CENTRE FOR ACADIAN STUDIES, UNIVERSITY OF MONCTON

Stephen White has written the definitive books on Acadian families, and through a lifetime of scholarship has been the central figure in reconstructing the divisions and disappearances that resulted from families being separated during the deportation. Getting an interview with Monsieur White at a Congrès mondial is like trying to get an interview with the pope at the Vatican during Easter. He is in constant demand to give speeches, sign books, a moment here, a moment there.

Everyone wants to talk to him. I managed to get a few minutes with him at breakfast when he explained just how he got started on the path to becoming Acadie's genealogist.

Stephen: I don't know how to explain it to most rational people. For me, it's always been not a job, but a sense of vocation, as if I've been called to it. I had a great-uncle who was interested in it and that helped. When I started college at Harvard, we went to visit him in West Arichat, which was where my grandparents were from. I was shown his work and the parish records and had the idea to continue the family research that he had begun. Then one of my cousins said, "You shouldn't ignore other families because everyone is related here," and that is more or less true.

The parish registers went back to 1839 and should have gone back to 1785, but the church had burned down. But because of my great-uncle's work I had older records. People saying it couldn't be done, that no one could reconstruct the history of all of the families, just made the task more of a challenge. I first went to the Centre acadien in Moncton in 1969, a year after it was founded, and there was more information there. I realized that with this new information I could bridge the gap between 1839 and 1785, and reconstruct the families in Cape Breton.

Father Anselme Chiasson [one of the founders of the Centre] had been carrying around two little notebooks in his pocket that had been given to him by the priest at Rivière Bourgeois. He didn't know what they were. They were in handwriting and a little messy, but it was clear to me that they were a record of mass intentions—a record of marriages to come, deaths to be remembered and so on. They were quite a find. I told him what they were and he gave them to me.

I had just begun working as a lawyer in the States. One day, the Centre offered me a job as staff genealogist. I didn't go looking for it; it came looking for me. One thing led to another and slowly we began to find the documents and talk to enough people that the story of the families began to be reconstructed. In the end, the study of genealogy is always about more than who's related to whom; it's about who was doing what, where they lived. Lines in the sand become paths, paths become roads, and you begin to see the character of individuals and the people. If you're a Savoie, you know that your family was part of a group of 150 Acadians that dug a tunnel out from under Fort Lawrence and escaped to travel north to freedom. If you're a Bourgeois, you know that Jacques Bourgeois was the founder of Beaubassin, the largest village in all of Acadie, a trader, entrepreneur, negotiator with the English. To this day, the Bourgeois are traders and entrepreneurs. If you're a Doucet, you know that you are not a big family like the Leblancs, but you are everywhere. Everywhere there are Acadians, there are Doucets. The Doucets really got scattered.

Clive: Does this information matter?

Stephen: Of course it does. History is just a fancy word for stories, and stories are about what happens to people.

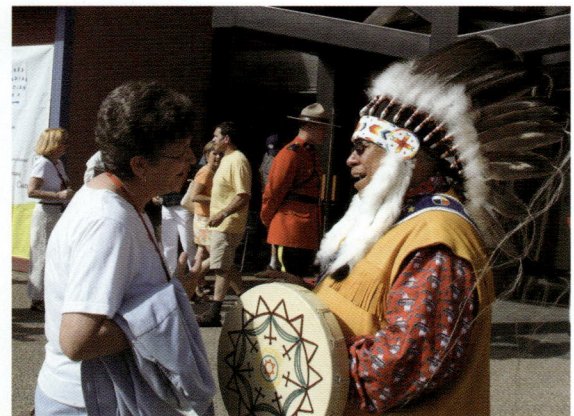

Mi'kmaw chief Frank Nivin welcomes visitors to the new interpretation centre at the Grand-Pré National Historic Site. The bond between the Mi'kmaq and Acadians is long-standing and harmonious.

Clive: And through genealogy we discover our stories, is that what you're saying?

Stephen: Exactly. The names don't just come down to us as words on scraps of paper. They almost always come attached with little bits of information, either directly or indirectly. The more you explore the genealogical tree, the more these little pieces of information gather; gradually, a picture of a people and their times emerges. For example, it now seems probable that your ancestor Captain Germain Doucet had several wives. Today, we might say he slept around. This is interesting information when we are thinking about the Mi'kmaw connections. It makes you think about some of those marriage dispensations that were so popular in early Acadie. Some of them were about moving Métis marriages into the Acadian family fold. It's a little piece of information but it confirms what is written elsewhere. There is an openness to relations between the Acadian and Mi'kmaw people which you don't see in New England, for example, where the Abenaki people were regarded not much differently than coyotes.

CONVERSATION WITH BURKE MACDONNELL AND GEORGETTE BURKE, CAPE BRETON

Georgette Burke: I'm an Acadian Burke from L'Ardoise, and my husband Burke is a MacDonnell from Sydney. Everyone asks us about our names so I might as well tell you right off the bat. Burke was named after his father's friend who was killed in the Second War. When Burke proposed, I said, "Yes, but I'm not giving up my name." After I said this, we walked along in silence for about a mile and I thought, "Well, that's torn it." But it was okay with Burke. He just needed a few moments to get used to the idea, so that's how we became a couple called Burke Macdonnell and Georgette Burke.

Burke MacDonnell: I worked for a long time on the MacDonnell family history and when I had it all in place back to Scotland, I asked Georgette if she would like it if I worked on her family tree. I told her not to expect much, that it takes several years to get started. She just smiled and gave me this internet address. I dialed in with a question, explaining who I was, the name of my wife, her parents, just some very basic stuff. The next night, that's twenty-four hours later, I dialed back into the address to see if there had been any response. I couldn't believe it. Pages and pages of stuff from all over the world. It was amazing—years of work in one day, from one letter.

3

EVANGELINE, GRAND-PRÉ, AND THE NATIONAL HISTORIC SITE

Your name is larger than Acadie,
More than the hopes of a homeland.
Your name carries past all borders.
Your name is the name of all those
Who, even though they be unhappy,
Believe in love and cling to hope.

– Last verse of the song
"Evangeline" by Michel Conte

Poets are central to every
nation's identity. Who can
imagine England without
Shakespeare, or France
without Molière? Their
plays and poems are now an
integral part of the foundation
of English and French

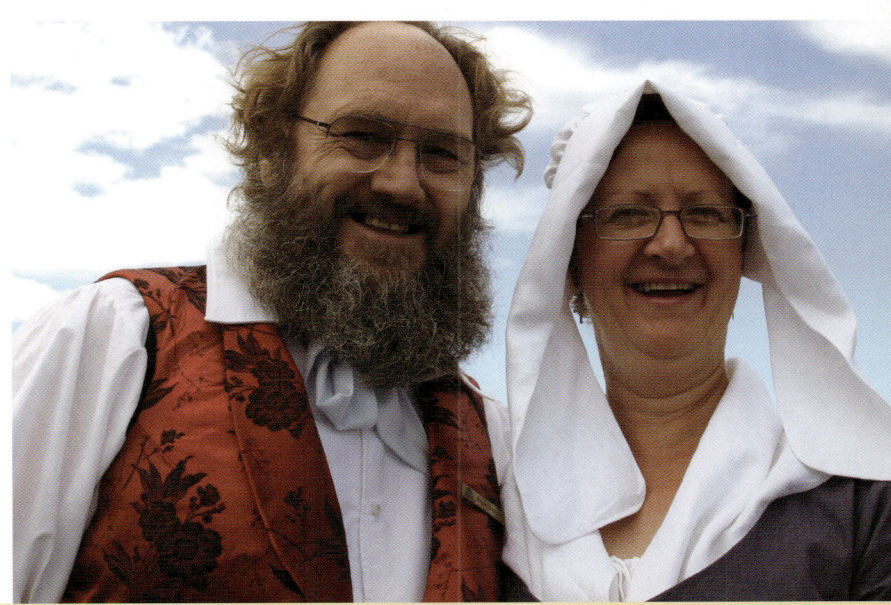

Two visitors straight from the past enjoy the pilgrimage in time and space at Grand-Pré. Roger Sevigny's period costume models the famous poet Longfellow, whereas Susan Surette-Draper's traditional costume reflects the dress of an Acadian woman in the 1700s.

character and language. But *Evangeline*, like the Acadians themselves, represents a unique literary phenomenon: this great anchoring narrative poem of the Acadian people, a poem that has had the enduring popularity of *Anne of Green Gables*, the mythical power of *Roland at Roncevaux*, wasn't written in Acadian French or even by an Acadian. Amazingly, it was written by an American, the poet Henry Wadsworth Longfellow—and both his heroine, Evangeline, and her lush birthplace, Grand-Pré, have become a defining metaphor for Acadie.

The many artistic manifestations of Evangeline are a poignant reminder of the heartbreak of the Acadian expulsion. In this photograph, taken from Evangeline, a musical drama directed by Normand Godin at the Marc-Lescarbot theatre, Gabriel searches for his love Evangeline.

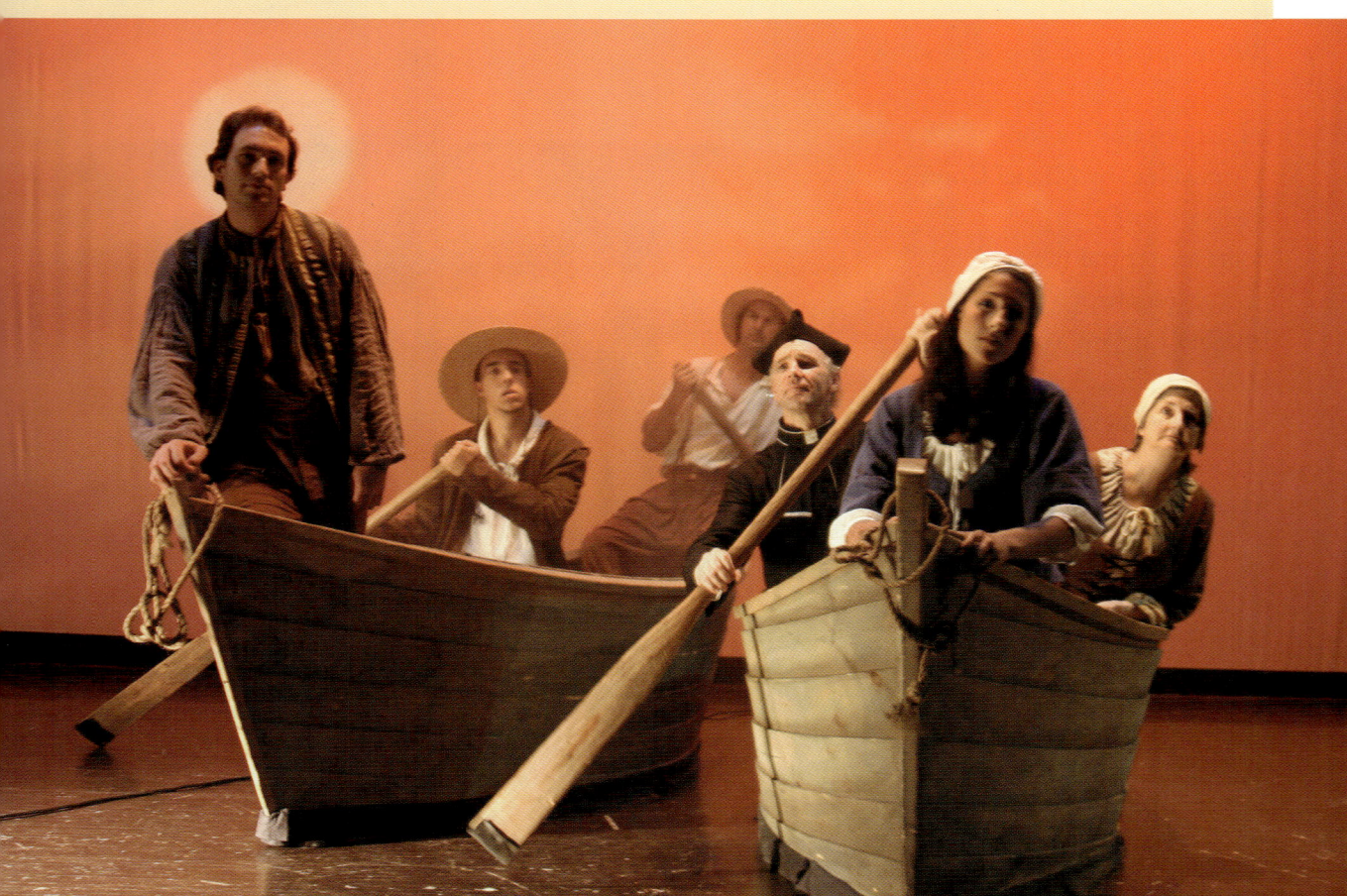

CONVERSATION WITH NORMAN GODIN, DIRECTOR OF THE MUSICAL EVANGELINE, UNIVERSITÉ SAINTE-ANNE

The Acadians have taken Evangeline as a symbol of their identity. Each year, communities all over Acadie choose an Evangeline and a Gabriel to represent their community. It is not imposed; it is the symbol Acadians themselves choose. When the poem is taken in its pure form, it a sad story, but we use the vitality and talent of the present-day generation to tell the story with such energy and passion that the poem gets turned on its head into a kind of triumph. We have had visitors from Korea and Yugoslavia who see the play and they've said they've lived similar events. From that turmoil, you react and make something of it and the Acadians have; that's the story of Evangeline today.

An eerie moment from the musical drama Evangeline captures the despair of Evangeline's eternal search for her lost lover, Gabriel.

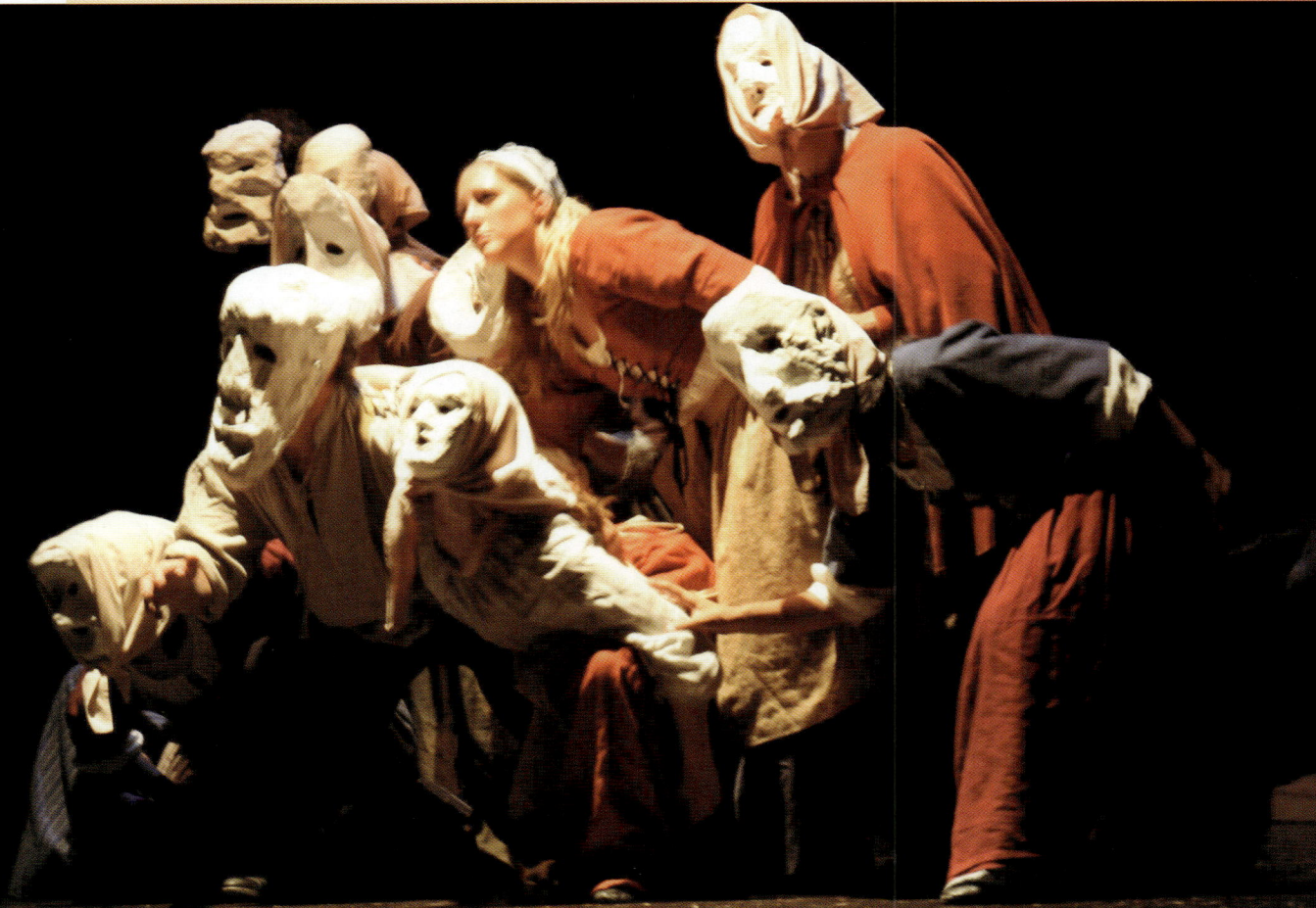

In choosing Grand-Pré as the site for his poem, Longfellow established the symbolic centre of the Acadian exile, which in turn played a vital role in the Acadian renaissance. Acadians all over the world now see Grand-Pré as their homeland, and events at the Congrès reflected that.

At the Grand-Pré Interpretation Centre, the parking lots were jammed from dawn until dusk. The spacious building was crammed with visitors attending exhibits, lectures, concerts and story-telling. Chief Daniel Paul read from his book *We Were Not the Savages*. There was traditional Mi'kmaw drumming. Theresa Meuse spoke about native spirituality, the medicine wheel and the sharing circle. Barbara Leblanc talked about her school program "Dancing Through the Centuries," which will be taught in Nova Scotia schools. In the program, children actually learn the dances of Acadian communities—in this way, the not only do children learn how to dance, but the experience teaches what the culture is about and how it evolved. Yvette Pitre from Rogersville told stories while dancers from Isle Madame performed. Warren Perrin, the Cajun lawyer and activist from Louisiana, talked about his petition for an apology from the Queen, which resulted in official recognition by the Canadian government of the deportation. Cajun and Acadian fiddlers performed together. Samuel Arsenault told the story of the transformation of the marshes across the centuries; Michel Tourete from France talked about the Acadian establishments in France after the deportation.

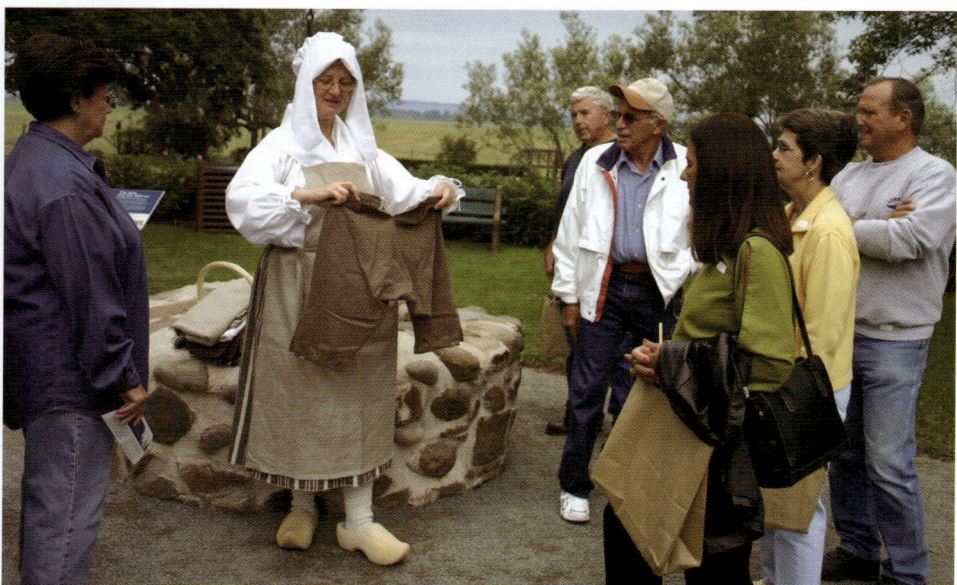

The busy two weeks of the Congrès were filled with family reunions. Susan Surette-Draper, dressed as Catherine Breau, displays seventeenth-century clothing to members of the Thibodeaux family.

I ended my visit by talking with two people deeply involved in the Grand-Pré site. It is truly remarkable that all of us were brought together by history and the power of a single poem.

CONVERSATION WITH JONATHAN FOWLER, ARCHAEOLOGIST, GRAND-PRÉ

I had been doing a lot of research in Acadian colonial history and Acadian–Mi'kmaw intermarriage. I got a copy of John Winslow's journal, and it's clear in the journal that his soldiers burnt hundreds of houses and barns. I began compiling a list of the houses burnt in the old villages and identifying the locations through air photographs. Then I began to get an idea of the extent of the habitations. This part of the province is just covered with signs of Acadian occupation. The sites have been destroyed, but they're still there. I'm digging right here because some workmen using a mechanical augur, augured right into a grave site.

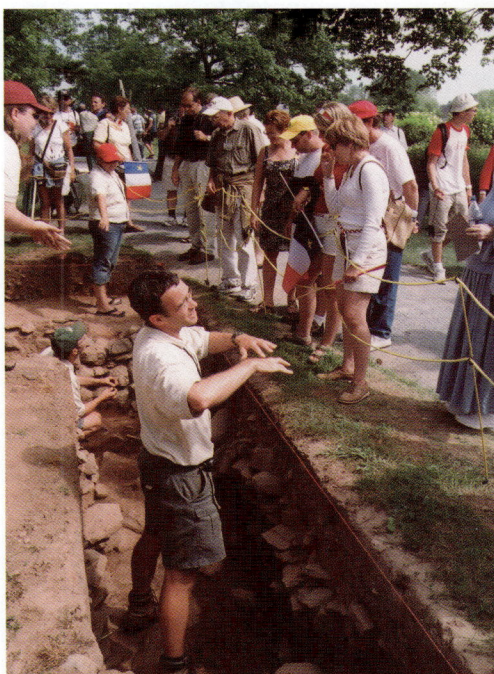

Archaeologist Jonathan Fowler explains his work to onlookers at Grand-Pré.

Before 1883, there were a lot of treasure hunters on the site. They exhumed coffins not far from where we are standing. A couple of them were put on display at the railway station and tourists just broke off bits and took them home as souvenirs, until there was nothing left. John Frederic Herbin is responsible for saving a small part of the old landscape for us today. His mother was an Acadian from Wedgeport; his father, a goldsmith from France. He built this stone cross to protect the site where the coffins had been pulled out and bought acreage with his own money to protect it from farming and development.

Herbin found what has always been thought to be the basement of St. Charles des Mines church, where the boys and men of Grand-Pré were imprisoned. It is where the present memorial church, built in 1922, stands; that's always been the official story, but we're no longer sure if it is the right one. In 1897, a David Otto Parker created a pamphlet to give the towns of Wolfville and Grand-Pré to sell to tourists. Unlike Herbin, he drew a map to scale and paced off the distance from the graves to what has always been known as Evangeline's well. We paced it off also and he was right on, but the electromagnetic pictures of Parker's position for the house and church don't reveal anything nearly big enough to house over 418 people, which is the number Winslow said he imprisoned. Plus, at the centre of the electromagnetic photograph, there's just a pile of rubble, which doesn't give much evidence that a structure of any grand dimension was there.

It gets weirder. Jeremiah Bancroft was Winslow's ensign; he also kept a journal, which we have as well as Winslow's. Winslow built a palisade around the church, the house and the graveyard. Bancroft recorded the dimensions as eighty-five metres by forty-five metres. It's a rectangular structure. If you take those dimensions and move them around Herbin's cross, which appears to be the site for the graveyard, you can't get any configuration which will take in where the church is supposed to be now. Parker was right about what he saw. He correctly paced off the distances between the graveyard and the well and what he thought were the ruins of the church. But which ruins are they? Remember, we're in the middle of a village. There are ruins in every direction. So where was the church? I don't think we know.

One of the things that strikes me when I read histories of Acadie is how well the political history is known. Historians can give you every detail about the Treaty of Paris, the Treaty of

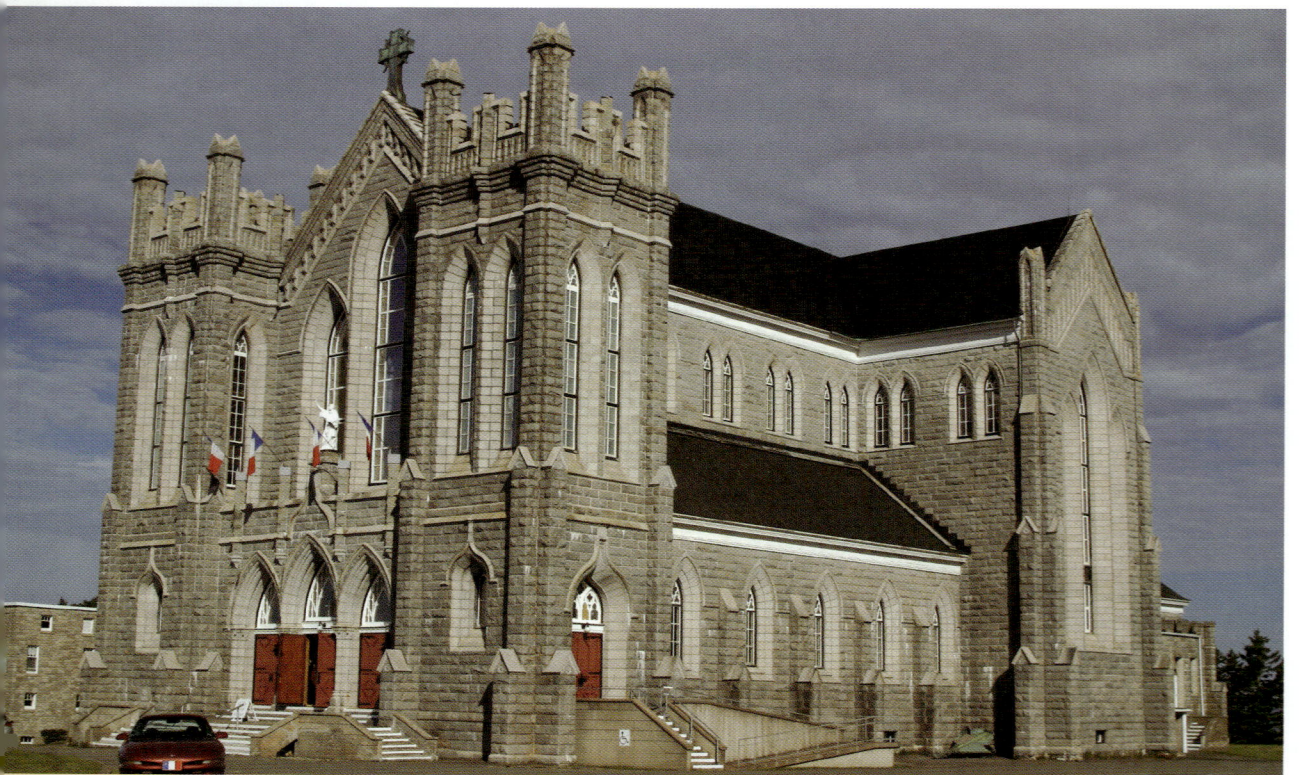

The magnificent Saint-Bernard church is an impressive construction of stone in the Saint-Bernard parish in Clare. The church's dignified structure is sacred to thousands of Acadians who still uphold the tradition of Roman Catholicism.

Utrecht, and so on, all of which affected the Acadians. They have also recorded every attempt to procure an oath of military allegiance from the Acadians from 1689 on. They know who was there, even what was said. But there is never much said about how people lived, what they were like. They had taverns as well as churches, expensive homes as well as cottages.

You can only understand the history of these people when you have walked where they walked. The picture that emerges from the archaeological evidence is fascinating. These were sophisticated people who understood their environment in a way that few ever do. We've found slates with holes drilled in them, which says to me that they probably slated some of their roofs, yet the image is always of thatched cottages. The closest place the slate could have come from is up in the South Mountain, ten to twenty kilometres away. And a friend of mine found a pipe bowl fragment in the interior of Nova Scotia, where few people travel even today. We could identify the pipe and its age because the pipe bowl had the maker's name on it. These kinds of distances tell you that these people traveled, and that they were profoundly connected to their environment.

You can't walk around here and not be impressed by the environment. In seventeenth and eighteenth-century terms, it did have an element of utopia about it. From Cape Blomidon to the Gaspereau River, there were thirty villages and three thousand people, five rivers like fingers cut down from the hills: the Perrault, the Habitant, the Canard, the Gaspereau, and the Grand Habitant. All of them retain their original Acadian names, with the exception of the Grand Habitant, which was renamed the Cornwallis River. Le vieux logis, now called Horton's Landing, was the site of both the first Acadian landing and the eventual deportation. You can't go down there and look out on three thousand acres, see the church spire in the distance—and you can see it from anywhere—and not be moved by how it all fits together. It's intricate. It's complicated. The fields, the dykes, the rivers, the villages—they all fit together.

Clive: Do you see the Acadians as submissive?

Jonathan: I see them as tremendously confident. They had such success here. Everyone who writes about Acadie writes about the agricultural wealth and the stubborn determination to be independent. No one bullied the Acadians; not the church, not France, not the Canadians, not the New Englanders. They set their own course. Cowed, fearful people aren't stubbornly independent—confident, successful people are. I walk this landscape and I see a people who must have thought they could prosper anywhere. My guess is that the pre-exile Acadians thought that as long as they could find a place where governments would leave them alone, no matter where it was, they could find a way to do well, because that had been their experience here. They had lived through wars, frequent attacks, pressure from all sides, and had still done well.

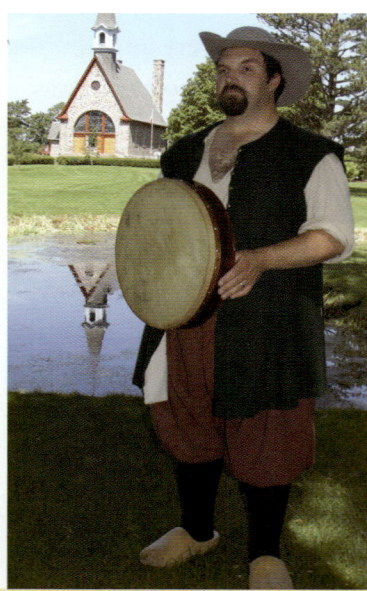

Mike Charlton in period costume charms visitors with a bodhran (an ancient single-headed frame drum) and his baritone voice. He stands by the pond of Grand-Pré, with the historic site's majestic souvenir church in the background.

Clive: But they didn't know that there was no possibility of finding a landscape like Grand-Pré, Minas, and Beaubassin?

Jonathan: That's right. In 1755, North America was still largely unexplored. No one could have known that the Bay of Fundy had the highest tides on the planet and North America's largest salt marshes. No, there is no other place like the tidal flats of the Bay of Fundy. They are unique, and the Acadians adapted to them in a unique way.

CONVERSATION WITH DONNA DOUCET, DIRECTOR, SOCIÉTÉ PROMOTION GRAND-PRÉ

When I started working in the interpretation centre, I didn't know anything about my culture. I didn't speak French. My parents put me in the English school system. My father's first language was French but he didn't speak French at home. I kept my maiden name when I got married, and it always bothered me that I didn't speak French. When my children were young, I began to listen to Passe-Partout on Radio-Canada. I found a job here at the interpretation centre and I began to take courses at the Université Sainte-Anne. I took history courses with Neil Boucher and education courses with Barbara Leblanc.

For a long time, Acadians have wanted a say in what should be constructed at Grand-Pré, and in 1985 a consultation committee was established to discuss how the site should be presented, managed, and what programs should be sponsored. The Société national des acadiens (SNA), the Fédération des acadiens de Nouvelle Écosse (FANE), and the consultation committee all began to promote the idea of co-management of the site. And in 1998, Parks Canada decided it wanted to reduce its costs and devolve some of its responsibilities to local organizations, so it was a good match. Barbara Leblanc was the first Parks Canada Director at Grand-Pré, and she was the first president of the Société promotion Grand-Pré, the Acadian half of the equation.

Our main focus from the beginning has been the creation of the interpretation centre. This is a five-million dollar project. It was a big undertaking. We raised money ourselves. We worked with Heritage Canada and Parks Canada. We pushed and pushed and finally it opened on August 15 of last year. It is a very big structure, filled with sunlight that cascades in from roof-high windows at both ends, down a broad, main concourse like a street, with a film theatre, a bookstore, lecture halls, and displays lining each side of the concourse. Since we opened it, the interpretation centre has made an enormous difference. It's an imposing, validating place to communicate our history. People are impressed even before they visit the rest of the site.

I grew up being ashamed of the Doucet name, and since I was ashamed of my name, I was also ashamed of who I was. When my father married an Irish Catholic, I think he considered it a step up; that's why he didn't speak French at home. He wanted us to blend in. I don't blame my father. When you've been treated like second-class citizens for a very long time—and that's mostly how Acadians were considered in Bathurst—it's hard not to think that you really are.

Working here in Grand-Pré, surrounded by Acadian history, I woke up to my culture, my language, my story. I learned that Acadians didn't build dykes because they were too lazy to cut down trees, which is what I learned in school, but because it was a unique, clever and successful thing that they had invented. I began to see the Acadian story with different eyes, with pride in what they had done, how they had always persevered against great odds.

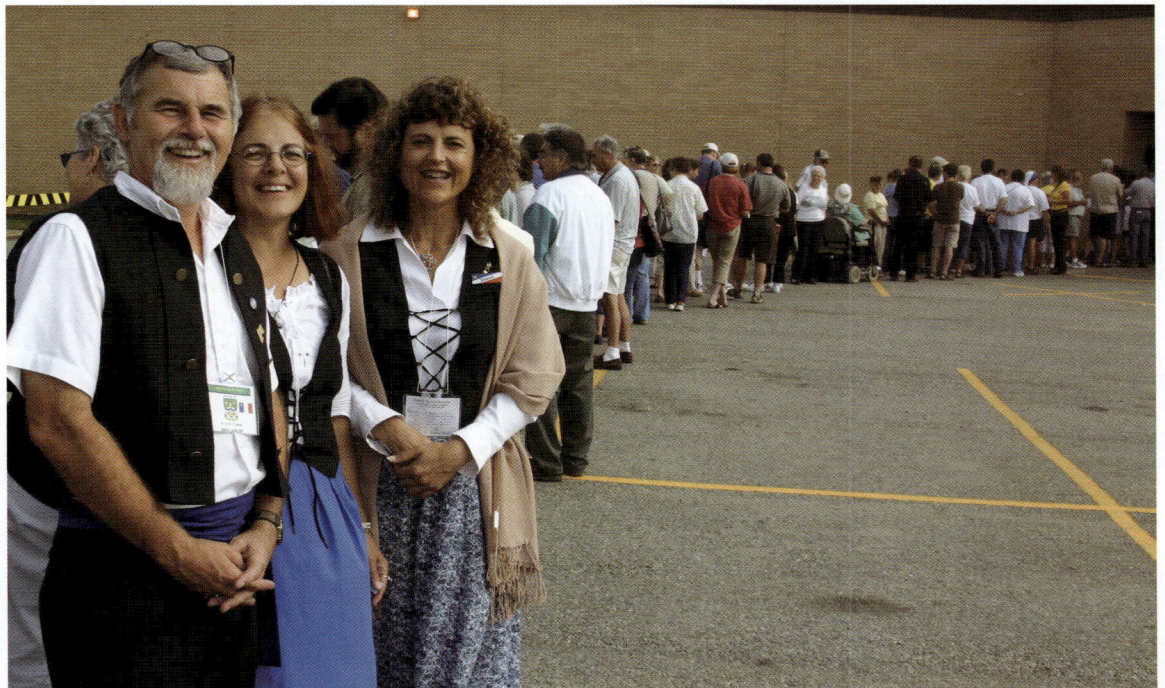

From left to right, Wayne Currie, Jeanne Doucet-Currie, and Pauline Doucet-Scott wait in line to attend an event at Saint-Anne University. The festive mood of such events helped make even waiting in line a chance to reconnect with old acquaintances and new friends.

4

FATHER ANSELME CHIASSON AND FATHER DANIEL BOUDREAU

Born in Chéticamp in 1911, Father Anselme Chiasson is revered as a pioneer in Acadian studies. He left Chéticamp and went to Ottawa to study before entering the priesthood in 1931. He was ordained in 1938 in Chéticamp. While studying in Ottawa, he began compiling notes on his home village, which eventually led to the publication of its history in 1961. Rev. Anselme Chiasson spent more than sixty years promoting Acadian culture and history through his research and his books. He was a member of the Order of Canada, L'Ordre des francophones d'Amérique and La médaille de chevalier de l'ordre national du merite, one of France's highest honours.

– From *Tribute to Rev. Anselme Chiasson*, by the local committee of the CMA 2004, Chéticamp.

There are two branches of the Catholic church: the executive branch, with its pope, cardinals, archbishops and bishops, and the working men and women's branch. Père Anselme Chiasson belonged to the second branch, one that I have always admired: that wonderful array of men and women who have unselfishly devoted their lives to trying to make the world a little better, as teachers, nurses, singers, historians, and companions on life's journey. Père Anselme died two months before the Congrès opened, an event in which he was slated to participate with his usual youthful vigour. He was ninety-two. His cousin, and co-author of many of his books, Father Daniel Boudreau, said, "He was only old for two weeks."

He would have been pleased to know that his memory was invoked many times at the Congrès. At the opening concert, he was remembered by the musical group 1755, the Beatles of Acadie, before they sang their last song. Father Daniel Boudreau gave a wonderful eulogy for him at the Mi-temps in Chéticamp. Edith Butler sang songs from his collection at her concert in Chéticamp. They were all fitting tributes. Fathers Chiasson and Boudreau were responsible for gathering together one of the world's greatest collections of traditional French songs that exists anywhere: more than 525 different songs in all.

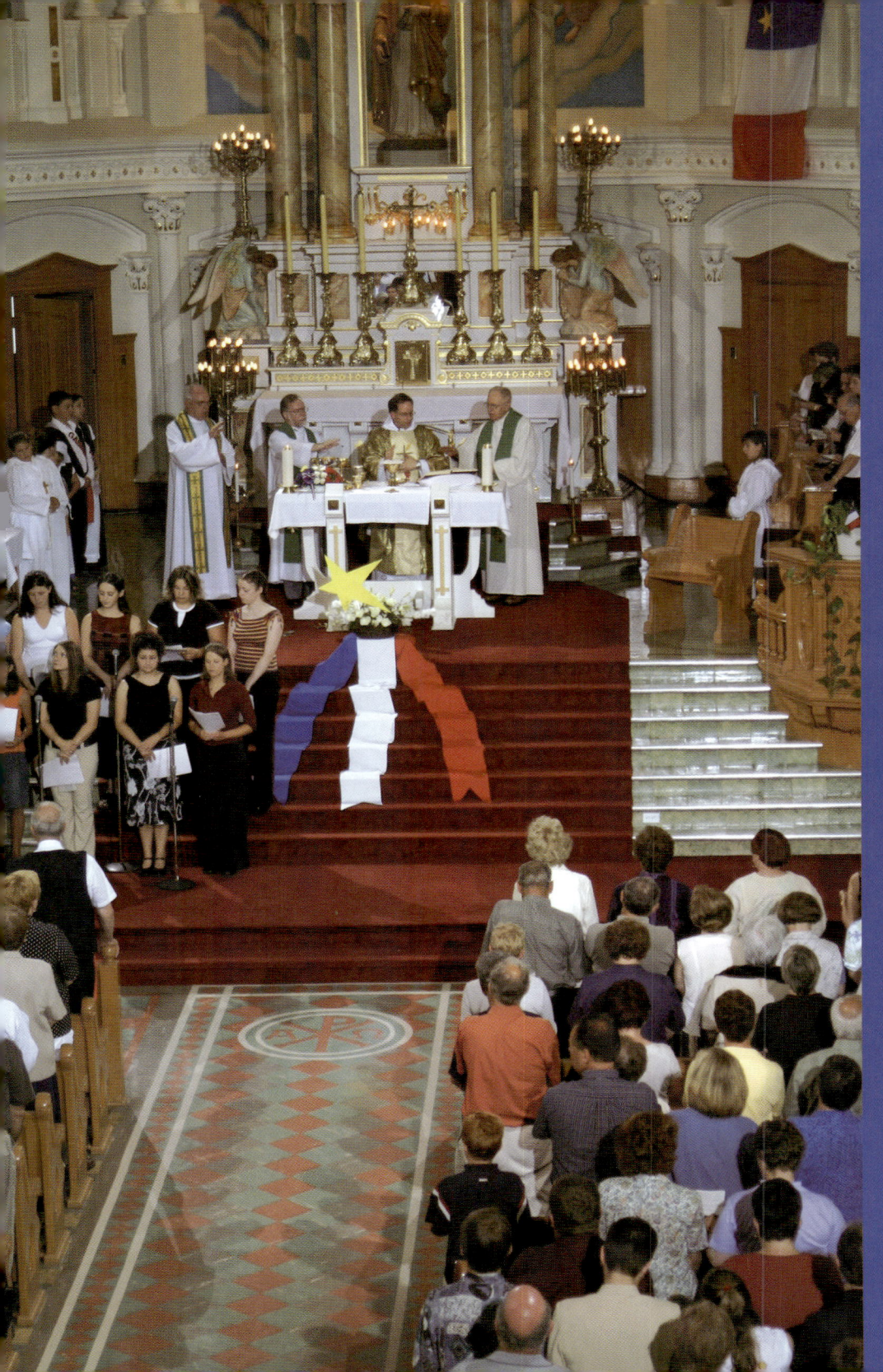

Mass at the Saint-Pierre Church in Cheticamp before the festival du mitan. The Baroque interior of the church is spectacular, with gold leaf detailing and an original Casavant organ dating from 1904. The church interior was redesigned in the 1980s in preparation for the upcoming Canadian centennial.

After centuries of very little being written by Acadians due to their oral culture, a literary explosion of poems, plays, novels, and histories has occurred in the last fifty years. Fifty years ago, Father Anselme was regarded as a little eccentric, the priest who cared more about old songs and old times than liturgy. Times change. Edith Butler's beautiful, new album *Madame Butlerfly* is composed entirely of traditional songs. There are now over four hundred books in the catalogue of Éditions d'Acadie alone. The bookshelves of the Congrès were groaning with new books from both French and English publishers. But Anselme Chiasson did something no other author did. He did not give his opinions or pronounce on the Acadian reality. He just wrote down what he saw and heard, and in the process created a library of musical and cultural information that will remain a precious resource for Acadie and the world.

Father Daniel Boudreau finished his eulogy by sitting down on a stool and singing in a fine, full voice one of the tunes that he and Father Anselme had collected, accompanied only by the beat kept by his hands and feet. Daniel Boudreau, at the age of eighty-two, has recorded every one of the songs that Anselme collected, and other talented elders, like Leo Cormier, have recorded traditional Acadian songs. So both the songs and the sound of a traditional delivery are being preserved.

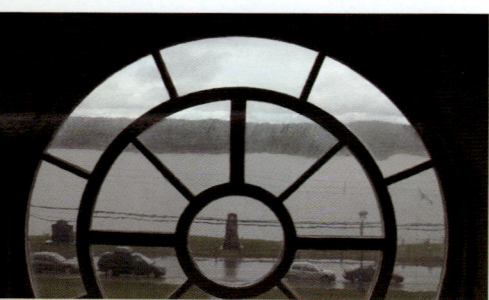

This photograph shows the view from inside Saint-Pierre Church. Built overlooking the harbour between 1892 and 1893, the construction of the Saint-Pierre Church was a community effort.

The spirit and accomplishments of Fathers Chiasson and Boudreau are exceptional. At the age of ninety, Father Chiasson drove from Moncton to the Magdalen Islands to take part in their Festival international contes en îles, then on to Chéticamp. He was one of the founders of the Centre d'études acadiennes and the Société historique acadienne. Both have become important institutions to Acadians. He touched more lives than he will ever know.

When I was a young student at the Université de Montréal, I met an ex-nun from Chéticamp. Her name was Estelle Cormier. I remember her name because it is on the name plate of the book that she gave me, Anselme Chiasson's *Chéticamp, histoire et traditions acadiennes*. It was the first time that I had ever read any book about Acadie. It's a very simple book, but I still refer to it from time to time, and I think of Estelle Cormier, who kindly gave it to me. I have tried to follow her example and pass on books to others. These gifts are without measure, for which we owe many thanks to Fathers Chiasson and Boudreau. It is right that Father Anselme was honoured as part of the Congrès.

5

Le Mi-temps, Chéticamp

The history of Chéticamp began after the deportation. Prior to 1755, there were no Mi'kmaw or Acadian settlements on the north shore of Cape Breton, but the deportation changed that. No longer a negative trait, Chéticamp's isolation meant that it was relatively safe for Acadian

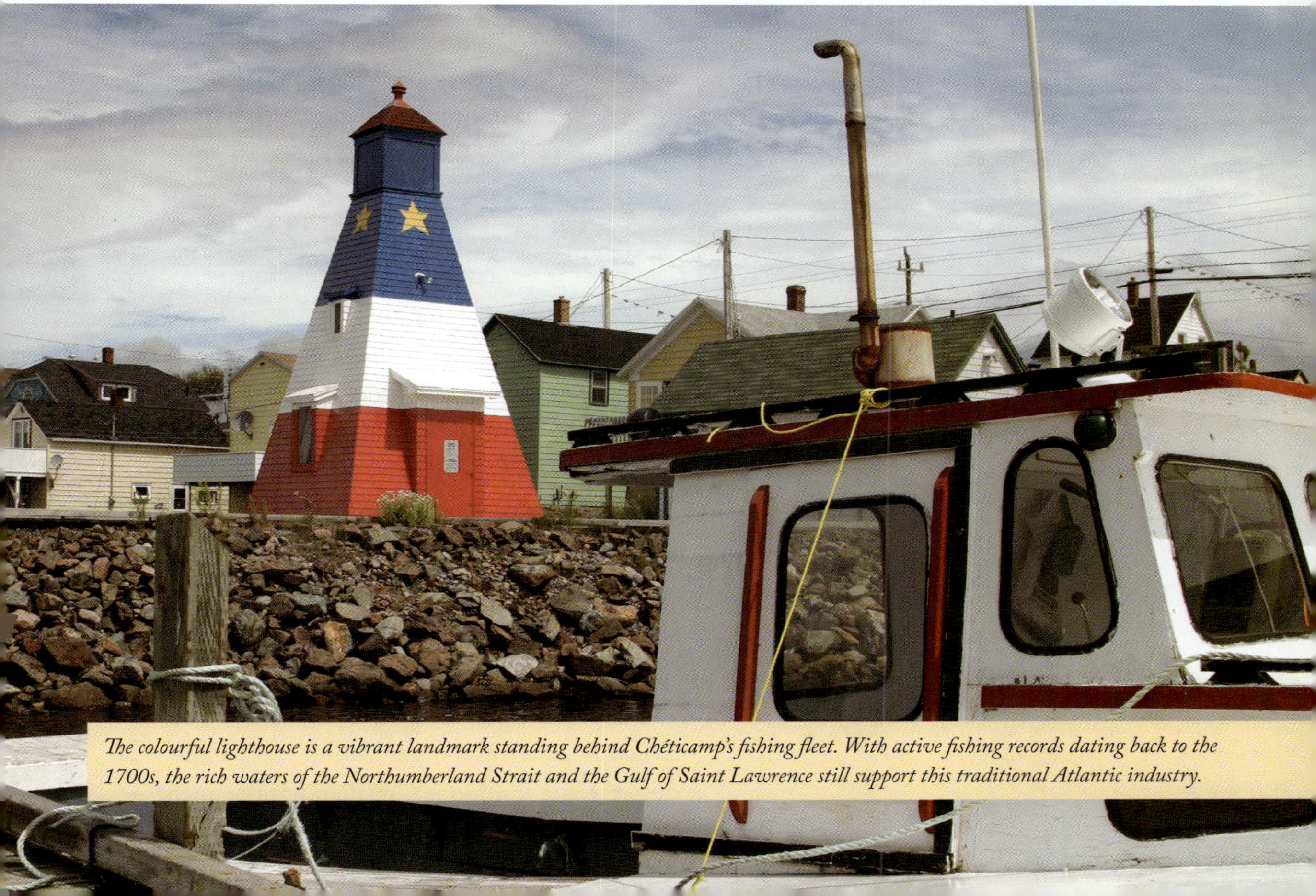

The colourful lighthouse is a vibrant landmark standing behind Chéticamp's fishing fleet. With active fishing records dating back to the 1700s, the rich waters of the Northumberland Strait and the Gulf of Saint Lawrence still support this traditional Atlantic industry.

refugees. French-speaking Protestant merchants from the Channel Island of Jersey recognized an opportunity in the refugees wandering along the coasts seeking shelter and work: there were rich fishing grounds off Chéticamp, but no one to catch and process the fish. The merchants petitioned the governor in Halifax to allow some Acadians to settle in the Chéticamp area, their petition was successful, and Acadians began to arrive from the four corners of the earth.

In 1782, twenty-seven years after the deportation began, there were still only two families in Chéticamp, but by 1790 there were twenty-six. These families felt confident enough to send a delegation of fourteen men to the government in Sydney, requesting a charter that would recognize their rights to the land. They were successful. A charter was granted, giving them legal ownership of the land they had settled in Chéticamp, and soon new Acadian villages stretched both north and south of Chéticamp—Belle Côte, Terre Noire, Grand Étang, Point Cross, Petit Étang, and Cap Rouge—and began to be settled.

As with the rest of the country, much has changed in Chéticamp and its surrounding communities in the past half-century. In some ways, though, the village has not changed at all. The spirit of economic and cultural independence is as lively as ever. Chéticamp and its neighbouring villages embraced the co-operative movement in the 1930s, becoming a hotbed of self-directed, community-owned societies embracing everything from the fish plant to crafts and culture. In this sense, nothing has changed. Today there are more than twenty co-operatives and non-profit organizations managing the radio station, day care, credit unions, life insurance companies, the cow pastures on Chéticamp Island, and the golf and outdoors clubs. The co-operative is a kind of economic and social organization particularly well-suited to the traditional Acadian temperament—

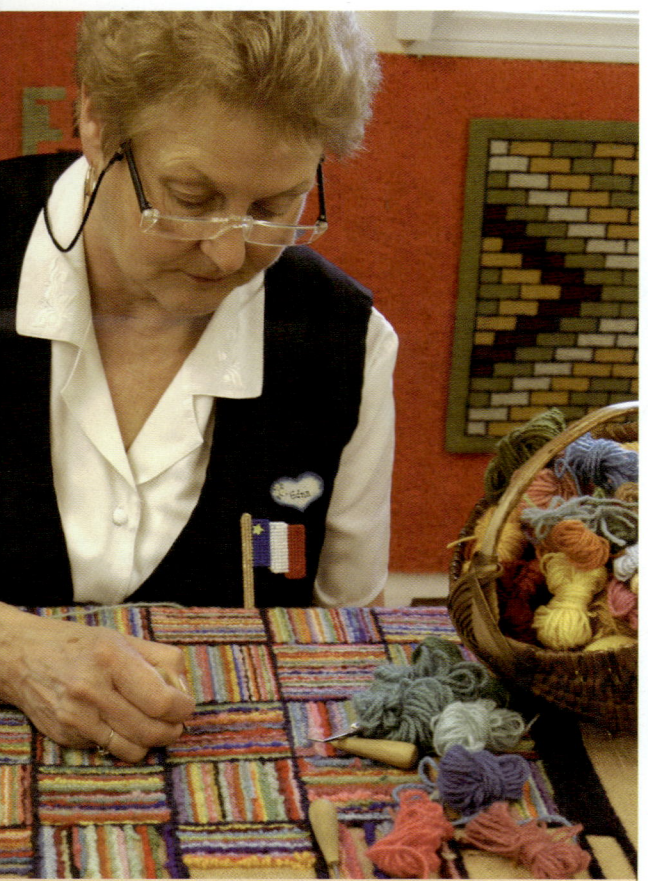

Edna Chiasson gives a lesson on the famous hooked rugs of Chéticamp. The tradition of rug-hooking is an important one to Acadian culture, and is kept alive by dedicated artisans who produce celebrated works of art.

their raison d'être is not individual profit, but community success by providing needed services for members. If profits do arise, they are divided among the members or reinvested in the organization in order to provide better services. Driving towards the village recently, I was listening to an interview with the director of the arts council, and I thought, "Isn't that great? The director of the Canada Council is visiting." At the end of the interview, the speaker was identified as Paul Gallant, the director of the Chéticamp Arts Council. It made me smile. How many other villages have their own arts council?

CONVERSATION WITH EDNA CHIASSON, ARTISANAT, CHÉTICAMP

I finished ninth grade, but nobody pushed me to go farther. I read a lot. I always have. I read both English and French. I don't get a chance to speak English much, so my pronunciation isn't as good as it could be, but I know all the words. My husband is a barber. We have two sons and now four grandchildren.

It's not necessary that we be all the same, that we all have the same words. The longer I work here the more certain I am of that. I don't like judgments. I don't find it pleasant when people say we speak chiac [a French-based language with many English and Mi'kmaw words, spoken around Moncton]. It's a

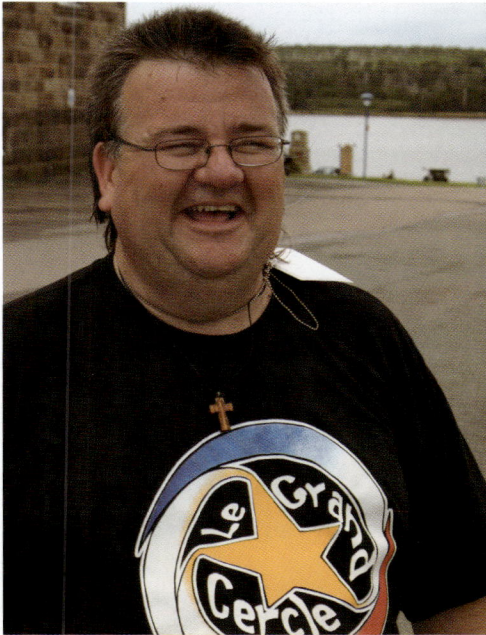

Paul Gallant, director of Grand Cercle, one of the main events of the festival du mitan, smiles for the camera. In the play, tradition meets modernity as the history of Acadie is depicted in a series of tableau which brought together over 250 local performers.

pressure just speaking. The Quebecois want you to sound like someone from Quebec. The French want you to sound like someone from France. I have Pascal Poirier's *Acadian Glossaire* at home, and I check it when I've used some words that a visitor doesn't understand. Sometimes it's in there and sometimes it isn't. For example, no one here says a *tasse de thé*; we say *une boulé de thé*. I've never seen it written down. Maybe it's *un bouilli*? I don't know. I just know it's not *une tasse*. It's fatiguing. Some days, it feels like I'm taking an exam every time I speak.

After I was married, I began to notice hooked rugs in people's homes. It began to interest me how an old piece of sacking could be transformed into something beautiful. By this time I had two children at home, and I finally took an evening course with Annie Rose Desveaux and her husband Gerard. I made some pieces and I put them on sale at the Artisanat. One day, someone from the Artisanat asked me if I would demonstrate some of the old *métiers* in the little museum we have here. I like people and I like to talk, so I thought, "Why not?"

At first, I was nervous, but I began to see people were really interested in what our parents and grandparents did out of necessity. If we wanted to have wool blankets, jackets, trousers and so on, we didn't buy them from China. The men raised the sheep, cut the wool, and carded it at the carding mill, and then the women spun it out on the spinning wheel and finally loomed it into material. We demonstrate the women's métiers here at the Artisanat.

I think the Congrès is really a good idea. It is good to see the people from Louisiana come and to be able to show them the country of our common origin. I always have this sense of being close to the people from Louisiana. It's more a feeling than any profound knowledge. Obviously, you can't really get to know anyone in a half-hour, but the sentiment is there. The dance, the music, la joie de vivre, one recognizes it in the Louisiannais.

We went through a difficult time with the school. Should it be French or not? I have two sons, and one was for a French school, one against. I don't see why we can't have a French school. If they can have French schools in Vancouver, why can't we here?

CONVERSATION WITH MAURICE POIRIER, LE HAVRE BOOK SHOP, CHÉTICAMP

Language and culture are held in the heart. If they are not there, then they're not anywhere. We've had this store for seventeen years. I've always played traditional music. I like to entertain. Bruno Bourgeois and I have sung together since we were in the seventh or eighth grade.

These last few years it has been much easier to be Acadian. There is more acceptance and we've got more tools to keep our culture. The community radio station and the Studio Marcel Doucet have really changed things. We can now hear our youngsters play on the radio. They can record. To have our own radio station in the village, I realize now, is not a luxury; it's a necessity. It's made a huge difference. The majority of people in the village listen to it. Radio-Canada is alright, but it's not us; CKJM is. Then there's the Collège d'Acadie at Grand Étang. All these things have made a difference.

CONVERSATION WITH NEIL MACDONALD, SCHOOL TEACHER, BELLE CÔTE

My dad is originally from Dingwall, on the other side of the island. He was in the merchant marine all his life, starting on the gypsum boats. He met my mum in Liverpool, England. She died in 1963 when I was eighteen months old. We came back to Canada to Dingwall in 1970 and I lived with my aunt and uncle because Dad was still at sea. Then we moved to Chéticamp in 1975 to stay with another uncle. I went to school in Chéticamp at NDA [Notre Dame de l'Assomption] from grade eight to twelve, then to St. Francis Xavier, and then to Teacher's College. I learned to understand French when I was teenager because all my friends were French, but I was too shy to speak it. When you're a kid, you're always afraid of being mocked.

In 1985–86, I was teaching in Winnipeg, and what should come on the national news, but Chéticamp and my old high school, NDA. There was some kind of bomb scare. Did that ever make me sit up. The whole community was divided. It was complex. It wasn't just about whether NDA should be only French or not. People were angry about the schools being amalgamated and losing their own village schools. Pleasant Bay and Chéticamp children were going to be separated and some of them were good

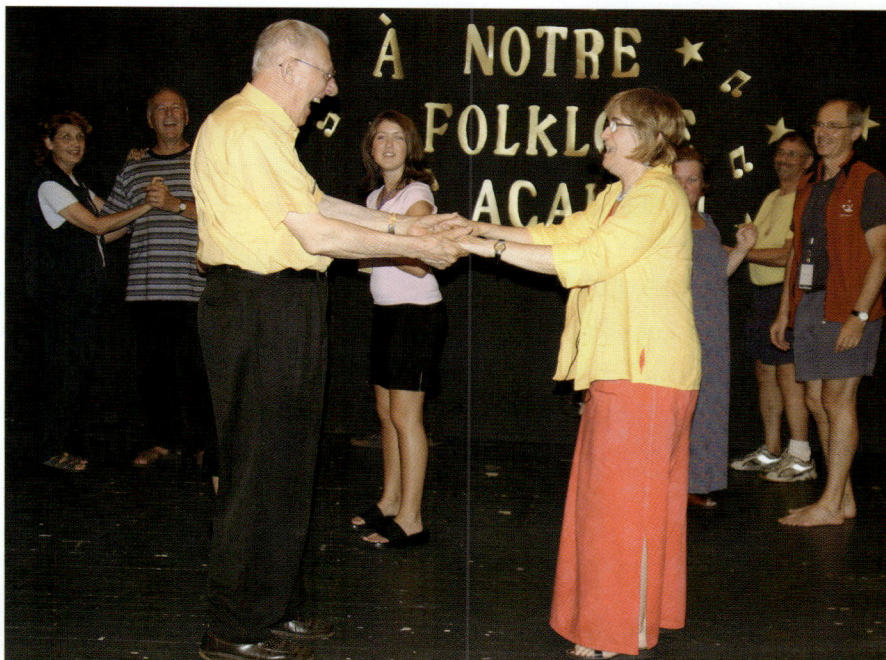

In Acadie's music-loving culture, dance is a natural pairing. Chéticamp's own Acadian powerhouse Barbara Leblanc teaches traditional folk dance steps to Father Daniel Boudreau, much to the enjoyment of the participants who discover dancing feet they didn't know they had.

friends. Then, there was the extra driving for the kids from Pleasant Bay to Belle Côte.

I teach at the new English school in Belle Côte, but my children go to NDA here in the village. Our daughter Terri was in Le grand cercle. My wife Polly Anne is from Chéticamp. You could say I've been adopted twice: once by the Scottish community and once by the Acadian.

CONVERSATION WITH BARBARA LEBLANC, AUTHOR AND EDUCATOR, CHÉTICAMP

Barbara Leblanc is a national treasure. When I met her for the first time in Moncton at the first Congrès mondial, she had recently obtained her doctorate from Laval in Acadian folklore, but what impressed me even more than her academic accomplishments was her zest for life. She had spent ten years in Italy in theatre, and one day was talking with her friends about their villages in Italy and the cultures of these places. It was then that Barbara realized that she also was from a village. She also had a culture. She also had a language, although one that she barely remembered because her parents had left St Joseph du Moine when she was only five and she hadn't spoken Acadian French for so many years.

She came home to find out what she had forgotten and where she was from. In her search, she has enriched us all. She became the first director of the Grand-Pré National Historic Site and the first director of the Société promotion Grand-Pré. She has written books like *Postcards from Acadie*, taught at the Université Sainte-Anne, and created new ways of learning history for students. Her latest project is a teaching guide for traditional Acadian dance in Nova Scotia schools. She has become a pillar not just of her family and friends, but of the Acadian people.

Barbara: Dance means different things in different cultures. In the Acadian culture, it is an expression of joy and of collectivity. I like the name for our dance program, Tous ensemble [all together], because that summarizes the way Acadie and Acadians have been. To survive in the New World wasn't easy. People worked together to build the dykes. They built houses together for new couples, and there was a certain equality between men and women as well as between

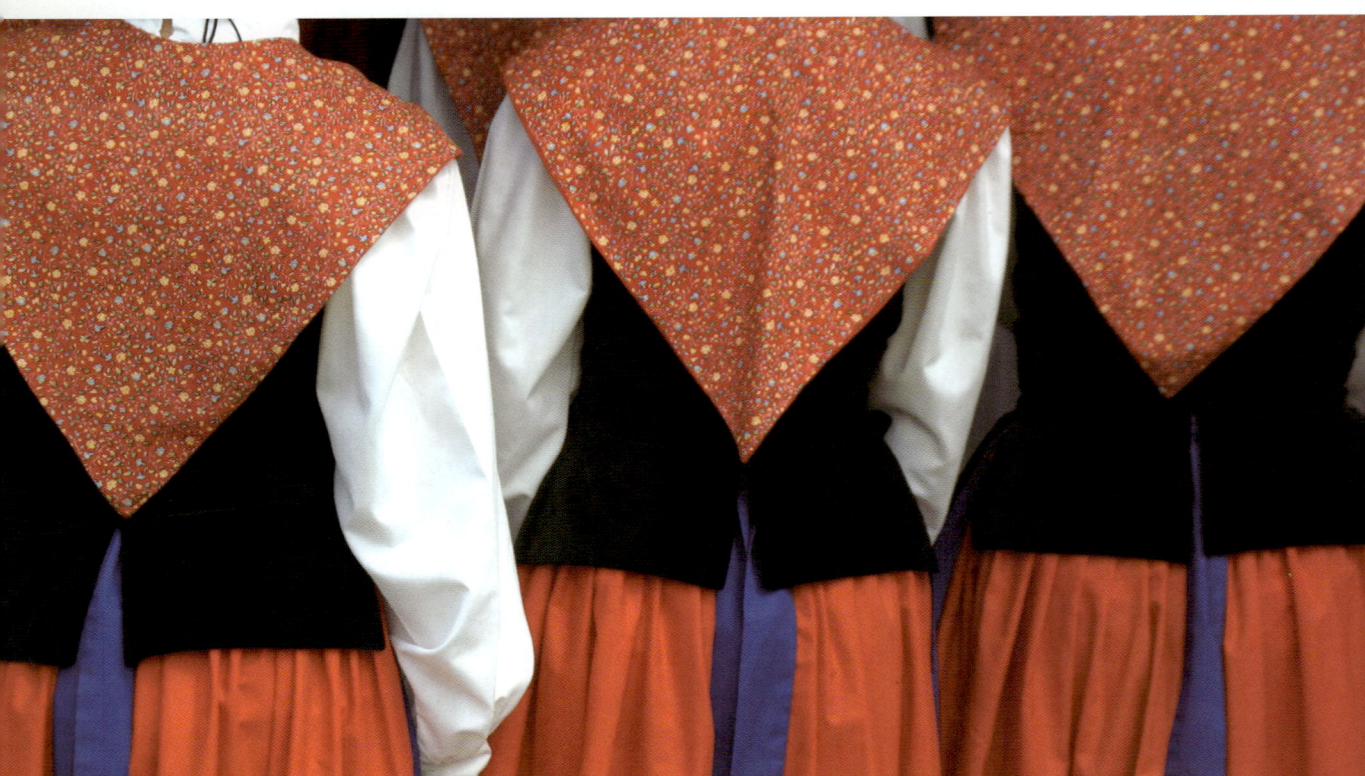

Decked out in full dancing attire, dancers from La baie en joie prepare to perform. The dance troop, comprised of Nova Scotia's finest young Acadian dancers, has achieved critical acclaim.

people generally. We see this in the oldest dances. There is an openness of spirit in the roles of men and women in the dance. Gender roles aren't as clearly defined as they become later. But for a dance to fly, everyone has to know the steps and the beat. A great evening of dancing isn't a solitary event with each person dancing in his or her own world. It is a collective act.

The program takes the students through the years from the earliest dances to now. Dance is always evolving, and it reflects the social forces of each generation. Today, individualism is the dominant social force. Each dancer does what he or she wishes. But it's a good thing to learn some of the dances of our ancestors, just like it's a good thing to have some old flowers in one's garden.

Each generation lets some dances fall away and invents others. Fortunately, because of Père Anselme we have the music. He saved the songs that Acadians have danced to for centuries. Before violin music was readily available, people would sing as they danced. They created the rhythms with their voices, and the movements of the dance with their bodies and feet. It was a complex, thoughtful act, the dance.

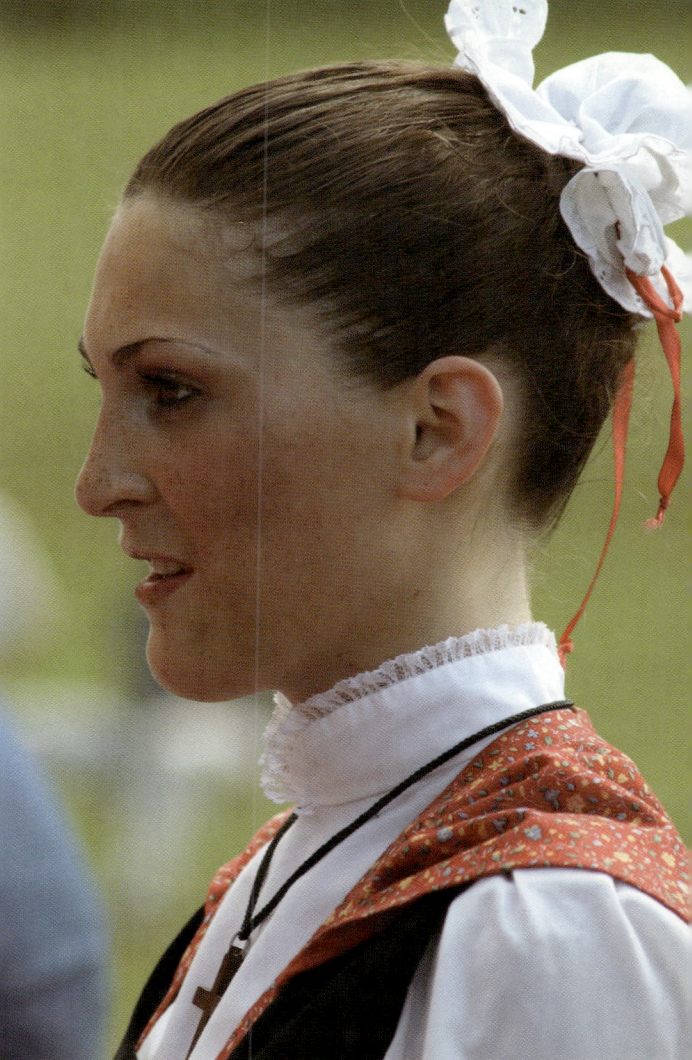

A side view of one of the talented La baie en joie dancers. The sophisticated choreography of the La baie en joie dancers and their rich costumes ensures their performances always delight.

I'm glad we're launching Tous ensemble at the Congrès mondial, because the Congrès is all about joining hands to celebrate community but still respecting diversity within and without the Acadian community. There is not one Acadie; there are many Acadies. The Acadie of Chéticamp is different from the Acadie of Baie Ste.-Marie. We should celebrate diversity without forgetting who we are.

6

MUSICIANS, WRITERS, AND VISUAL ARTISTS

Ubi Saltatio, ibi diabolis.
Où se trouve la danse, se trouve le diable.
Where one finds the dance, one finds the devil.

— Saint Jean Chrysostome, from Dance Nova Scotia's Guide to Traditional Acadian
Dances for Schools

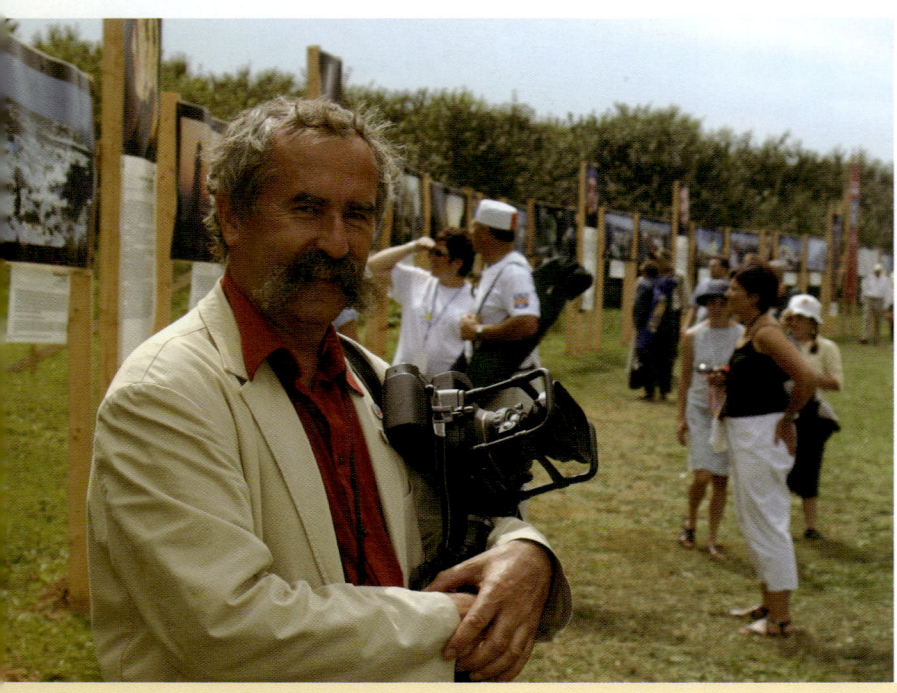

French photographer François Poche stands in front of his massive exposition, an Homage to Acadie on the grounds of the Grand-Pré National Historic Site.

Music and musicians have always been part of Acadie, both before the exile and after. The best indication of this is in the complaints of priests, which are as old as Acadie. As far back as the 1690s, priests complained that Acadian taverns remained open during Mass on Sundays, and Pierre Milliard, a missionary, wrote that the Mi'kmaq were better Catholics than the inhabitants. Two hundred and fifty years later, Father De

Coste in Grand Étang complained about the midwinter festival, the Chandeleur; eventually it was banned because it was too rowdy. There are well-known stories in Louisiana of people getting off the deportation boats and setting up a dance on the harbour dock. "The devil is in the dance," priests have been known to say, but that has never stopped Acadians from dancing.

When there was no violin or musical accompaniment available, people sang a cappella, using only the beat of the hand or the foot to keep time. The tradition of unaccompanied dance music lasted well into the twentieth century. In Chéticamp around 1940, Joe Cormier's father made a violin from a picture he had seen and a model that he took measurements from in Margaree. Joe went on to become a famous fiddler in Waltham, Massachusetts, playing at the French social club, making records, and performing in concerts all over North America.

By the 1950s, there were more violins in the villages of Grand Étang and Chéticamp, but the supply did not yet equal the demand. My cousin Marcel played at his first dance when he was eight years old and continued to play at dances and fêtes of every kind all his life.

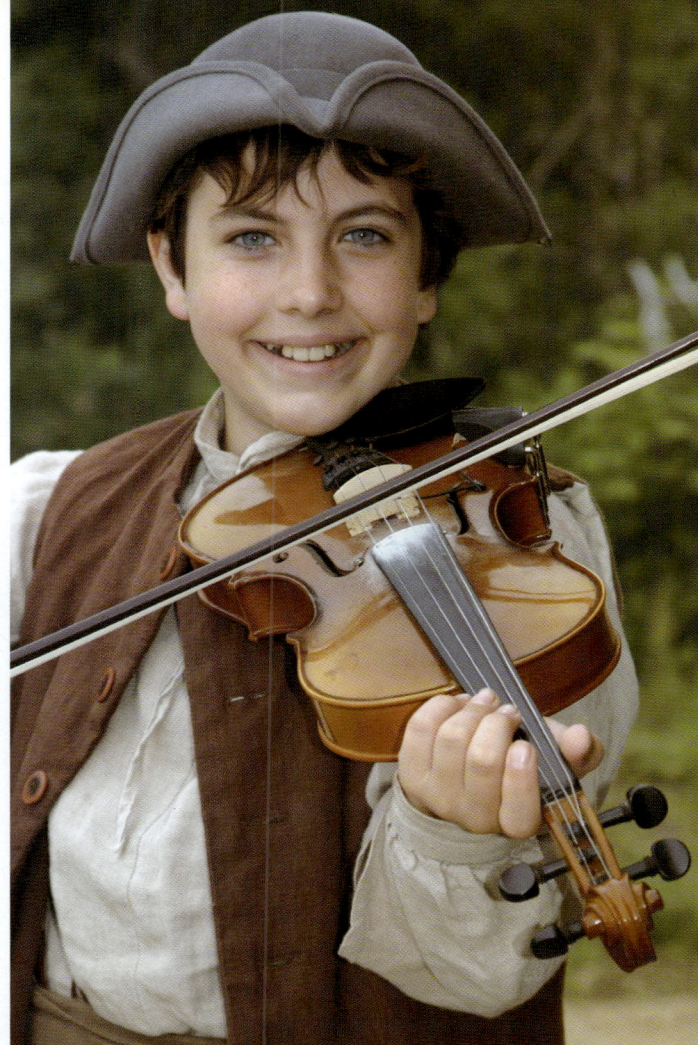

Dressed in traditional Acadian costume, young fiddler Leon Stuart is all smiles during a break from the play Evangeline.

Today, musicians and their violins are still a treasured commodity, but there are now more violin players in one music class in Chéticamp than there used to be on the entire Acadian shore.

To hear some of the great artists of Acadie performing is an unforgettable experience. There's a hum in the air as if the audience were vibrating along with the singers. Edith Butler sang her heart out at the Mi-temps concert in Chéticamp. I couldn't imagine a finer performance. The old songs flowed out on the wings of her magnificent voice, but it was not just her voice that the audience was hearing. We had the sense that the evening was imprinted with the very culture of our ancestors. This unspoken understanding gave the evening a thrilling energy.

An argument can be made that the finest fusion music in the world is Acadian, because it combines Creole and African traditions from Louisiana, Celtic traditions of Nova Scotia, and both French and European folk music, creating vibrant genres like Zydeco and Acadico.

Writers and visual artists occupy a very different place on the Acadian stage. Both are very new to Acadian society. Although much is made of the Order of Good Cheer and the New World's first theatrical productions by Marc Lescarbot at Port-Royal in the winter of 1606, there is very little written by Acadians before the 1970s. There are no plays, no poems, no novels, no memoirs.

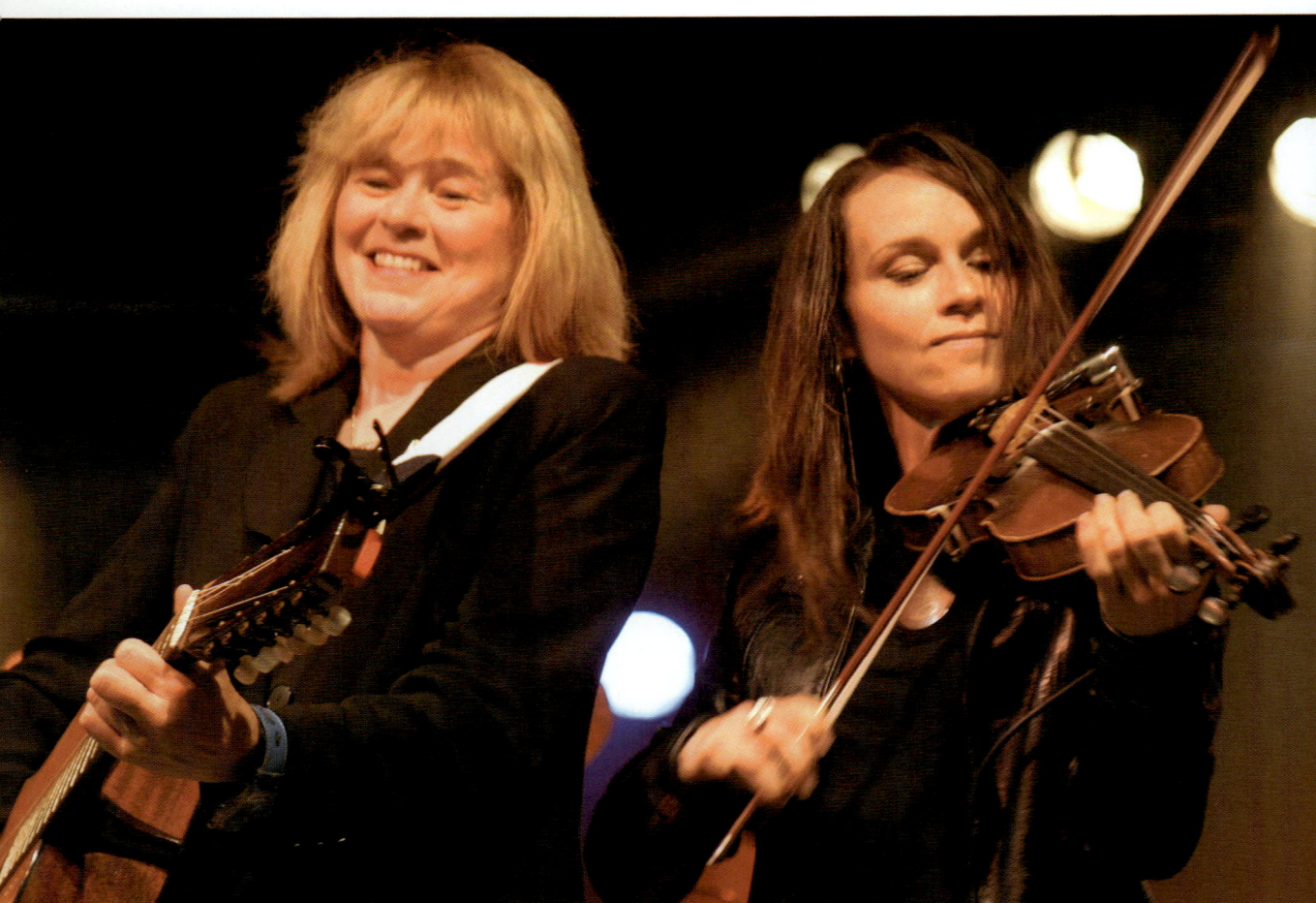

Ambassador of Acadian culture and traditions Edith Butler and her fiddle player perform at the Cabot Trail Arena. A variety of performers, ranging from blues legend Patrick Verbeke to the popular Grand Dérangement, came to the festival du mitan, a three-day Acadian cultural extravaganza.

It is very difficult to find any letters written between Acadians even during the wandering years. There are odd bits and pieces written about Acadie, mostly by census takers, missionaries, and the French and English militaries, from which a rough outline of Acadian history has been cobbled together.

There is Nicolas Denys's informative and sympathetic 1672 historical and geographical account of Acadie drawn from his many years there. There is a letter from a resident of Louisbourg, written in 1745, and a letter written in 1757 about the deportation and dispersion of the Acadians by François Le Guerne. There is Winslow's famous diary account of his part in the deportation. But mostly there is literary absence. There are no books, no traditions of Acadian reading, writing, or publishing. What men and women could do with their hands was what counted.

Around the time of Confederation, Acadie took its first small steps towards a literary society. Newspapers started appearing. In 1867, *Le moniteur acadien* was published in Shédiac by Israel Landry; in 1887 *L'Evangeline* was published out of Digby, Nova Scotia; and in 1893, *L'Impartial* appeared in Tignish, Prince

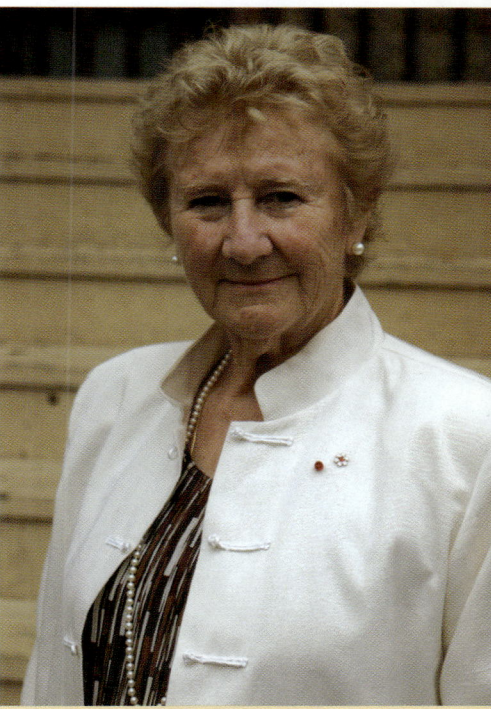

Acadian writer Antonine Maillet was a guest speaker at the academic conference.

Edward Island. Pascal Poirier was appointed to the Senate and began gathering material on the Acadian language that would eventually become his famous Acadian glossary, the first attempt to codify the particularities of Acadian French. In the 1960s, Anselme Chiasson began to publish his famous collections of legends, stories, songs, and village histories of Atlantic Canada. But all of these newspapers and books were exceptional efforts, and not representative of a literary tradition.

In 1971, all of this changed. Antonine Maillet's play *La Sagouine* appeared and began its incredibly successful run in Acadie, Quebec, and France. *La Sagouine* was not only a remarkable play, but the beginning of Acadian literature. Maillet followed this great success with a number of works, one of which, *Pélagie-la-Charette*, won France's Goncourt literary prize in 1979. She was the first Canadian distinguished in this way. In the thirty-five years since the publication of *La Sagouine*, an avalanche of poems, novels, and plays have poured from the pens of Acadian writers into Acadian communities and beyond.

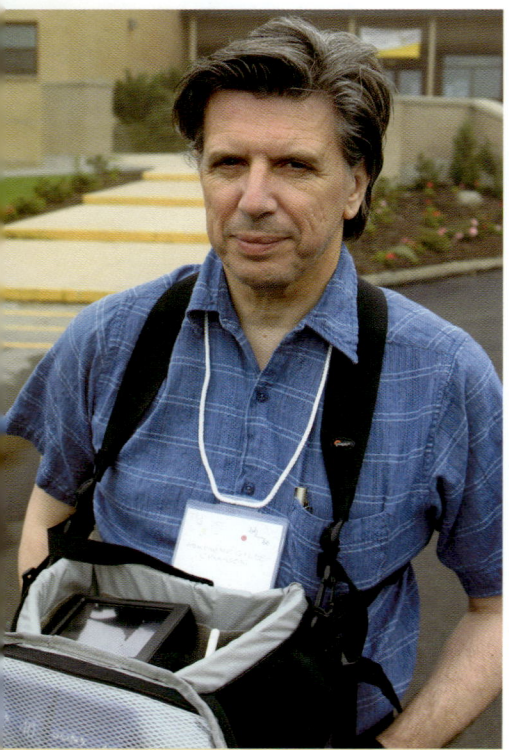

Herménégilde Chiasson attends the academic conference at Sainte-Anne University. Chiasson is a notable Acadian artist and writer living in New Brunswick. One of his ten published books won the Governor General's Award for poetry in 1999, and he has written many plays, directed films, and is a proficient painter. He is the lieutenant-governor of New Brunswick.

In 2004, there is a community not only of Acadian writers, but also Acadian publishing houses, theatres, and professional organizations, the institutional fabric so necessary in sustaining a literary culture. But writers are still a long way from having the pride of place that Acadian musicians do. It is not that they are less important, but Acadian stories are still told primarily via music, dance, and word of mouth. It is still not a culture that has codified itself in the pages of books as the French and English have. So, although there were many poets circulating at the Congrès—Herménégilde Chiasson was there representing the province of New Brunswick, and Antonine Maillet and Barry Jean Ancelet spoke at the academic conference—there were no nights of poetry, few readings, and fewer plays presented. This effervescent corner of Acadian society remains a quiet presence on the cultural stage, leaving the dominant roles to others.

In contrast, visual artists like Marcelle Belliveau said, "We're everywhere." Present at the Art Gallery of Nova Scotia were Romeo Savoie, Paul Edouard Bourque, François Gaudet, Herménegilde Chiasson, Denise Comeau, and Yvon Gallant. As with Acadian literature, the Acadian artistic sensibility has evolved incredibly quickly. In 1900, there was nothing, not a single image, that could be described as an Acadian painting. Then a French-Canadian painter, Henri Breau (1863–1949), inspired by—what else?—Longfellow's *Evangeline*, painted an enormous eight-by-ten-foot depiction of the deportation at Horton's Landing. In it, we see British soldiers, the transports in the bay, and Evangeline and her father sitting close to the centre of the painting, looking stunned and alone. Breau's painting is expertly rendered, but it is the subject matter that was exceptional. At the International Universal Exposition of 1900, held in Paris, Breau won a bronze medal.

The effect of this painting on the Acadian community was electric. The painting was valued at five thousand dollars at a time when annual incomes were only a few thousand, sometimes only a few hundred, dollars. But funds were raised in Acadian and New England parishes, and the

Société national de l'Acadie and the Société Saint Jean-Baptiste committed to contributions; not only was the five thousand dollars raised, but there was a surplus. For more information on this phenomenon, read *Postcards from Acadie*, by Barbara Leblanc.

Breau's painting marked the beginning of an Acadian visual arts scene. Within a very few years, Acadians themselves were painting, beginning with primitive and traditional oil techniques. In 2004, Acadian artists are creating art in every style—from two-dimensional naive painting styles to multi-media projects.

Born in 1920, Nelson Surette began painting using just his fingers. He became so adept at this technique that he kept using it, switching to paint brushes only for the finishing touches. Towards the end of his life, he created a magnificent series of paintings using the Acadian exile as theme. During the Congrès, Myra Freeman, lieutenant-governor of Nova Scotia, exhibited these paintings and some of the tapestries of Elizabeth Lefort at her residence in Halifax. Surette was a reclusive artist, and his paintings have not been readily available for public viewing, which made the Congrès exhibit that much more special.

CONVERSATION WITH DENISE COMEAU, PAINTER, BAIE STE.-MARIE

Denise Comeau began her successful artistic career creating realistic, finely rendered scenes from around her home in Baie Ste.-Marie—the house and lively laundry line of a neighbour, a butter-yellow dory floating on silver water, an Acadian flag flying from a porch. Her paintings all show a sharp eye for an evocative scene combined with an accomplished technical skill. But her latest paintings are abstracts—dark, dense creations that have no particular form, but that evoke for me the idea of a black hole, a negative space.

Denise: I know that I can create realistic scenes that will sell. I've done it. The abstracts come from another place. I think they have something to do with anger. Living in a situation where you are constantly reminded that your language and culture are in a minority position is a strain. It does bother

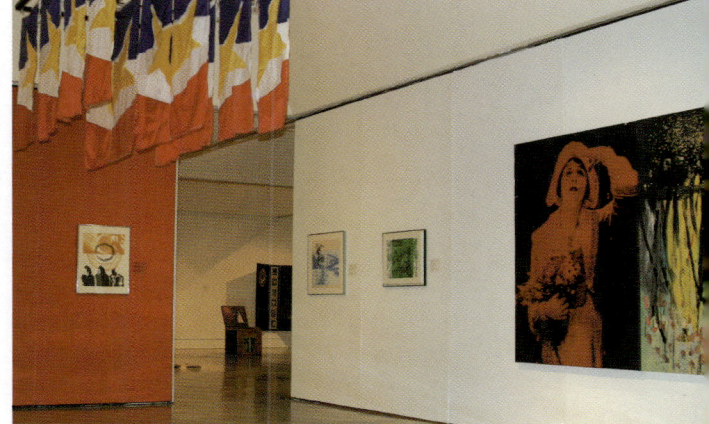

In celebration of the Congrès, the Art Gallery of Nova Scotia exhibited "Acadie Monde," which explored "identity in Acadian contemporary art." The show, which ran at the gallery from July to September 2004, showcased the creative works of Acadian artists and was curated by Moncton artist Mario Doucette.

me when I phone up a friend and she is a Francophone married to a Francophone but her phone message is entirely in English, as if she didn't speak French. It bothers me when I see two Francophones talking in English to each other in a restaurant. There's an element of cultural suicide in all of this, and I think these feelings come out in my abstracts.

The abstracts don't sell well. I feel disappointed. On the other hand, suppressing these feelings to make pretty pictures isn't such a good idea either. Maybe I'll find a middle ground sometime. I don't know what that would be but it would be interesting to find out—if I could ever bring the two sources of my paintings together to create something different.

An example of one of Elizabeth Lefort's rugs. Ms. Lefort has been distinguished as a Member of the Order of Canada, and her rugs can be viewed at the Vatican, the White House, the Museum of Civilization in Ottawa, and Buckingham Palace.

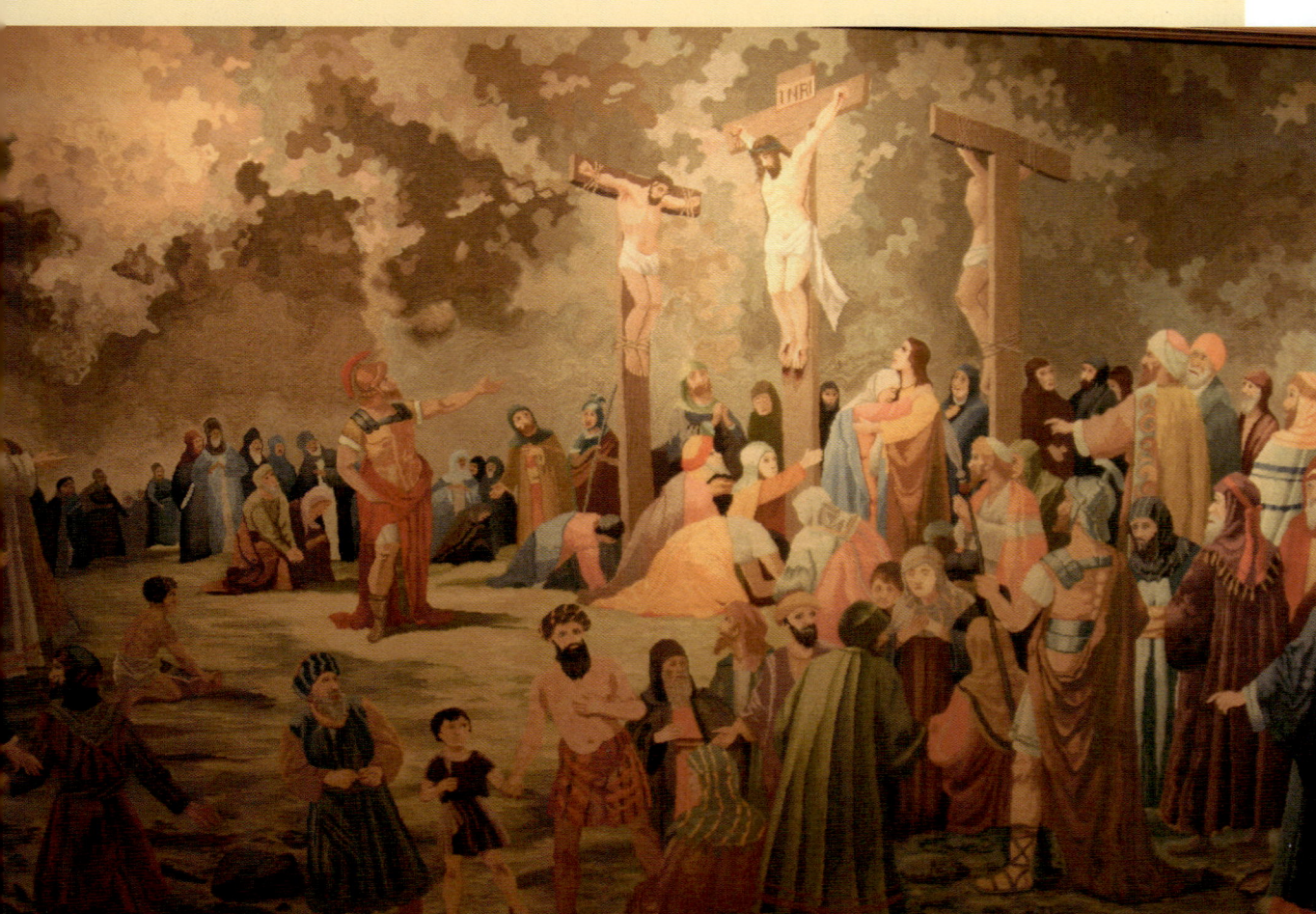

The Acadian artists of 2004 are looking at Evangeline and the deportation with fresh, innovative, challenging eyes, different eyes than those of previous generations. Breau would not recognize their images because they speak to a sensibility that just wasn't present in 1900.

CONVERSATION WITH WILLIAM ROACH, SCULPTOR AND PAINTER, PETIT ÉTANG

I started drawing with a pencil at four years old. My mother was also artistic, so it was always an interest. I left the village when I was fifteen and worked mostly in London, Ontario. I did all kinds of jobs: crane operating, dry cleaning, truck driving, construction work, fork-lift operating. When I wanted a change, I changed jobs. I painted on the weekends. But life in the city didn't work for me. It seemed like everyone was a robot. I couldn't find value to life and began to drink and do dope.

I came back to Petit Étang twenty-three years ago. I'm fifty-four now. I gave up the alcohol and the dope when I came back. The Kinsmen gave me a low-rent house, the one I am in now. They charged me twenty-five percent of what I could earn. I began to sell my art from my basement and through art dealers. I worked eight years unloading boats as a longshoreman, but eventually my back gave out and the doctor told me to leave it alone and just do my art. He said I could get a disability pension, but I refused. I wanted to live independently.

You're not allowed to set up a business in a low-rent house. I had to quit my art or quit the house; that's what I was told. So I borrowed some money from the bank and bought the house. I have three sons: Jason is a musician, Randy, an electrical engineer, and Robbie, an industrial electrician. They all learned the arts very young. My work is in the Smithsonian in Washington, the Nova Scotia Art Gallery, and other places.

The Congrès has widened my vision of Acadie and our history, but I can't say it's been much good for my business. People don't have much money or patience for art. Most of them don't seem to understand how long it takes to create even a simple sculpture.

CONVERSATION WITH ELIZABETH LEFORT, RUG HOOKER, MARGAREE HARBOUR

The Chéticamp region is famous for its hooked rugs; as a traditional winter pastime women created rugs by hooking wool through the tiny squares of old potato sacking until a patterned rug was formed. Two women were responsible for turning rug-hooking from a winter pastime into an art form. When Liliane Burke, an American with Acadian roots, first saw the hooked rugs of Chéticamp, she realized their marketing potential and began to buy the rugs up and sell them in Boston. At the same time, she pushed the Chéticamp women to create more sophisticated designs and use more complex arrangements of colours. One of these women, Elizabeth Lefort, became a genius of tapis hooké. Mechanically, she can hook twice as fast as anyone else, but it is her ability to create designs and portraits that is uncanny, almost eerie in its perfection. She has been to the White House twice and her portraits of US presidents Eisenhower and Johnson are so lifelike, it is difficult to believe that they are not photographs. Her use of colour and composition are more subtle than in an oil painting. There is a permanent gallery devoted to her art at Les Trois Pignons in Chéticamp. In 1987, she was made a member of the Order of Canada. She now lives in Margaree in a small white house overlooking the valley with a friend. At the time I talked with her, she was ninety.

Elizabeth: I began making hooked rugs for the floor. In all of our houses, the floors were made of wood, and in winter, they were cold. So we made wool rugs for the floors, especially at the edge of the bed. Then when you got out of bed with your bare feet in winter, they would touch the warm wool rug.

I was born in 1914 and began making rugs in the 1930s. It was the Depression and no one had anything. Everything that we needed to live was grown by the men or caught in the sea, and everything needed for the house was made by the women. If you want something now, you go to the Co-op and buy it, but when I was young we lived differently; we had no choice. If you didn't make your own rug, you had no rug. If you didn't churn your own butter, there was no butter. If you didn't make your own bread, there was no bread. If the men didn't salt away enough fish and put hay in the barn for the cows, the family went hungry. That was the way it was.

The Last Supper [one of Lefort's most famous hooked rugs] has 750,000 stitches in it. It has eleven kilometres of yarn, 416 colours and took me eight months to finish. Do you think anyone will do such a rug again?

CONVERSATION WITH MICHEL WILLIATTE-BATTET, SCULPTER AND PAINTER, STE. JOSEPH-DU-MOINE

I grew up in Quebec. The beauty of the countryside is what first attracted me to Nova Scotia: the sea, the geography. I had travelled for a considerable time and this is the place I decided I wanted to live. I am not Acadian,

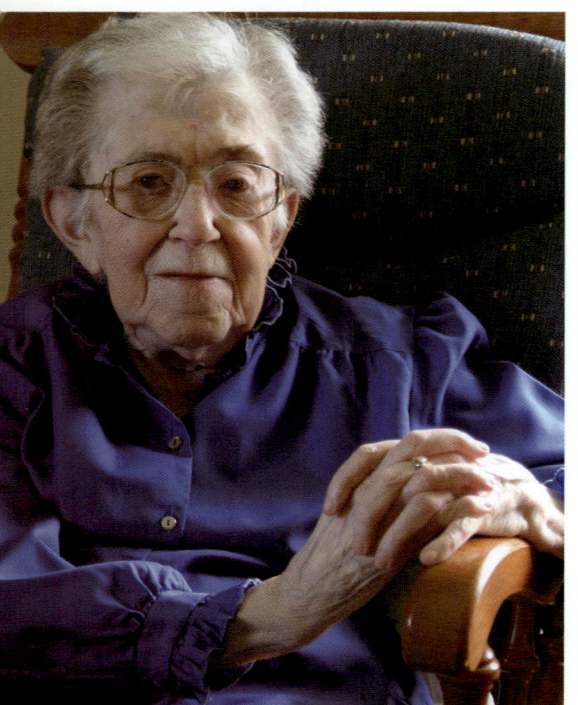

Elizabeth Lefort is a world-renowned rug hooker.

but there is an Acadian expression which applies to me: "Nous sommes venus pour rester [We came to stay]."

When I first came, people were a little suspicious. I think they worried that I would not be able to pay my bills, but once they realize you can pay your bills and you're serious, the welcome is very warm. I have a little farm. I keep chickens and goats. I give away the eggs in exchange for other services, especially the plowing of the lane in the winter. In the morning, you can hear my rooster crow across the barnyard. Sometimes on a very clear morning, you can hear the rooster of Michel Aucoin from the other end of the village answering. There is something very simple and reassuring in that sound.

I have this art gallery on the main road where I show my own artwork and that of others. It's my fifteenth year here. I am an autodidact. If you asked me why I am an artist, I could not tell you. My wife works as an assistant pastry chef in a restaurant. We have three little girls and an eleven-month-old. My wife is from Peterborough, but we will send the girls to French school. It is important to me that they speak French.

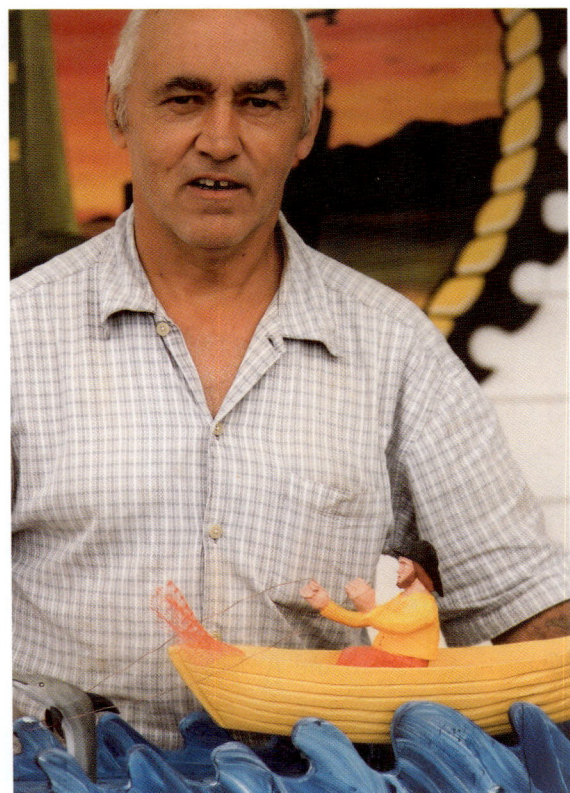

William Roach,
sculptor and painter, Petit Étang

7

YOUTH ASSEMBLY AND WOMEN'S SUMMIT

Youth Assembly, Mount Saint Vincent University, Halifax

STEPHANIE GAUDET, 21, BELLEVUE, SASKATCHEWAN

My great-great-grandfather left the Maritimes in 1860 for Quebec, and then their children, my great-grandparents, left for Saskatchewan in 1882. They were some of the first settlers in Bellevue. I am a fourteenth-generation Acadian and the fifth generation since we left Acadie. My grandparents are retired now and my parents do the farming. There are four girls in our family; three of them are at the Congrès. The fourth would be here, but she is too young. In Bellevue, half of the population is descended from people who first came to Port-Royal in Nova Scotia. We have a French school. The village has kept its language and traditions.

I want to be a teacher and I hope to teach my students the different aspects of the Francophone culture in North America. The Congrès is an excellent way to meet people, learn about our history, and experience our culture.

GUY GALLANT, 19, WELLINGTON, PRINCE EDWARD ISLAND

There are five thousand Acadians on Prince Edward Island, but I've been lucky enough to have my travel to all the different villages and regions of the Maritimes paid for by the SNA [Société national des acadiens]. My grandmother who just died, Jeanne Mance Arsenault, had a big influence on me and many others. She always worked hard to make sure we didn't lose our sense of ourselves as Acadians. For me, the Acadian flag is a signal to the world that I am Acadian and I belong to these people. The Acadian flag is about a history together, a culture, a language, une joie de vivre, but I see this flag in a different sense than the Canadian and American flags. They are more about territory.

REMI LEGER, 21, CAP-PELÉ, NEW BRUNSWICK

I am here with the political wing of the Fédération jeunesse canadienne-française. We organize a parliament each year. This will be the first one in Nova Scotia and we will be arguing several bills. The one I'm most interested in is a bill about the deportation, with arguments for and against. The British had reason to fear the Acadian presence because they were always at war with the French and the Acadians were of French descent. On the other hand, the Acadians were British subjects by virtue of international treaty and were neutral in the conflicts. So who was right? For me, Acadie is the three Maritime provinces.

I attended the academic conference at Church Point. There were four people in my session. I'm not sure we need an academic conference. Maybe we should let it go at the next Congrès.

Youth isn't just about tomorrow. We don't have the experience of older people, but we have something to contribute today.

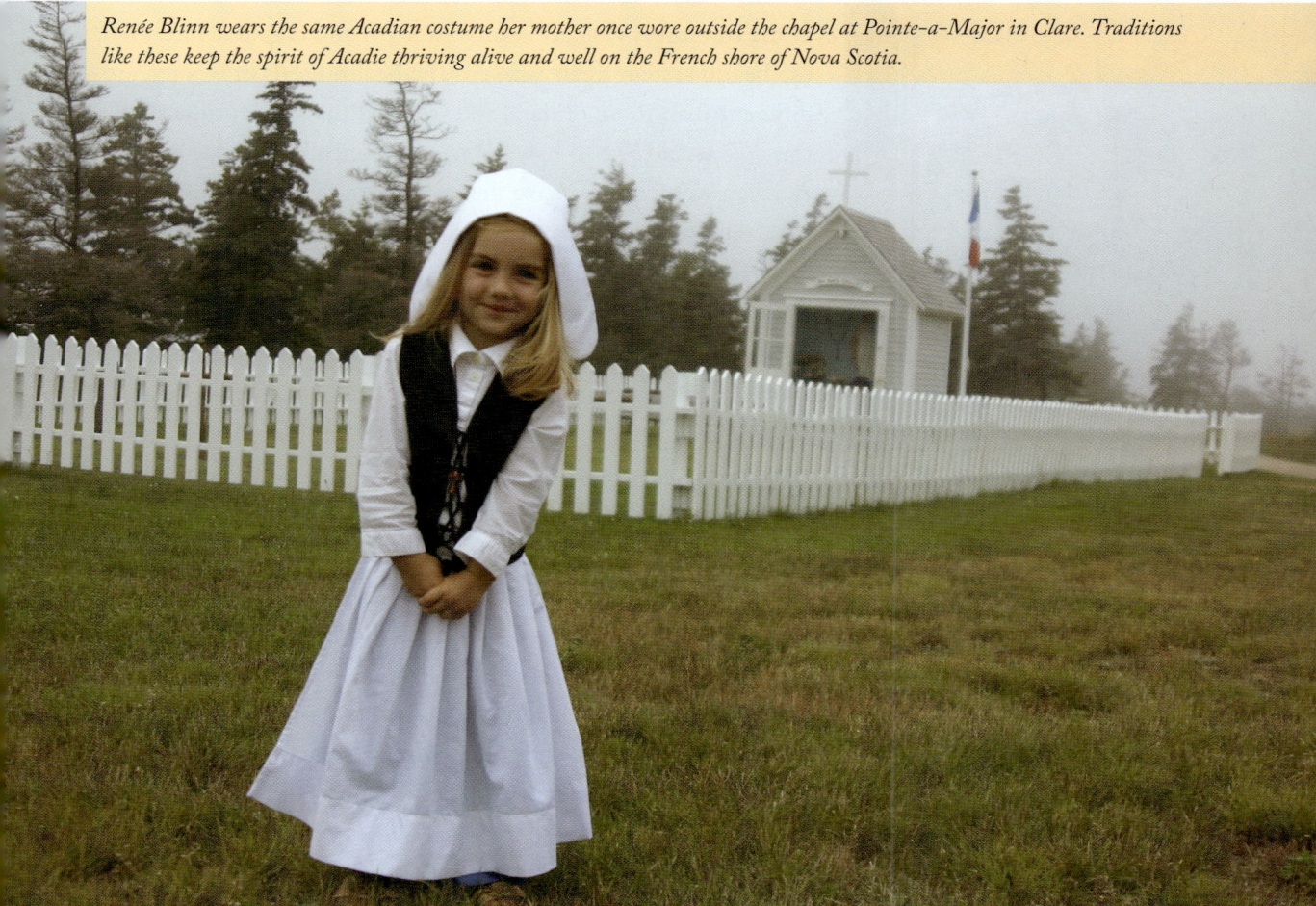

Renée Blinn wears the same Acadian costume her mother once wore outside the chapel at Pointe-a-Major in Clare. Traditions like these keep the spirit of Acadie thriving alive and well on the French shore of Nova Scotia.

VERONIQUE AND CATHERINE KINNEY, 14 AND 16, DARTMOUTH, NOVA SCOTIA

We live in Dartmouth, so it's very easy to get here—just twenty minutes. We go to a French school called Le Carrefour. We're here to make some new friends and to learn about the lives of others. The Acadians are a people who are really strong, who work well together, who are still here after four hundred years.

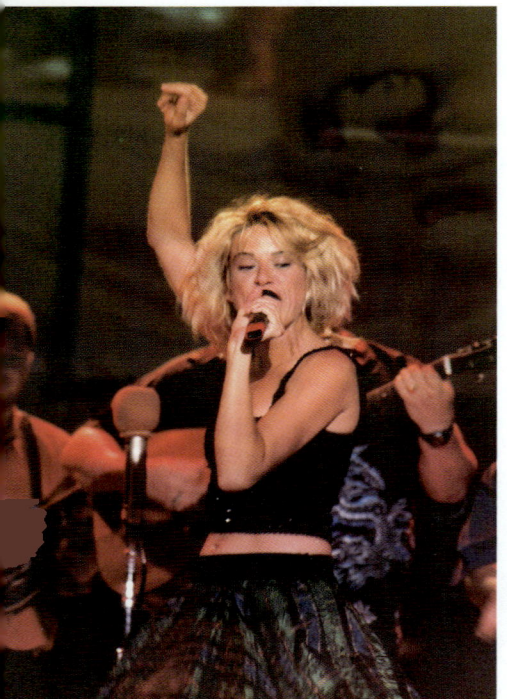

Marie Jo Thériault performs at the closing concert, Citadel Hill.

The Women's Summit, Holiday Inn, Dartmouth

LAURETTE DEVEAU, PRESIDENT OF WOMEN'S SUMMIT, PETIT ÉTANG

I come to Halifax once a year for meetings. The rest of the time I am in Petit Étang, about a kilometre from the entrance of the Cape Breton Highlands National Park. What we are focusing on at the summit is violence against women and children and how the health system treats women. The health needs of women are different than those of men, and we need the system to recognize this. We would like to have service in French because often Acadian women don't have the confidence that they should have in dealing with their problems in a context outside of the home. They are often dependent on parents' husbands when they are younger, and children when they are older.

At the summit, we are talking about the importance of women developing more confidence and autonomy, especially economic autonomy. With younger women this is a little easier because they are more flexible. We encourage young women to stay in school and study mathematics and the sciences in order to develop the right qualifications for the workplace.

I have confidence in the future. I think younger women are becoming much better educated and are developing careers where they can be independent. But it's another story with a woman in her forties or fifties.

I work for the Acadian Co-operative Council in Chéticamp. Our group tries to develop the co-op movement to keep it growing and responding to the changing needs of the community. Fishing is all but over now. All that is left is lobster, crab, and herring. If that goes, I don't know what the men will be able to do. We lost the Fishing Co-op; the men just couldn't make a go of it anymore. It isn't easy. Co-ops take community solidarity and a belief in the community, not profit. It's easy enough to make a success of a business. If there's a profit in it, you do it; if there isn't, you don't. There's no profit to be made in daycare, but it's needed by our community so we put together a daycare group and it's working.

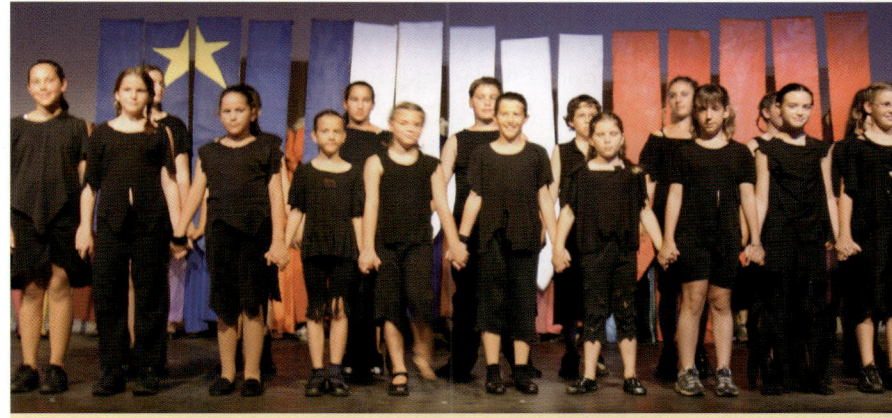

Young performers line up in front of an Acadian flag in this scene from the Grand Cercle production.

If the community is strong, normally the co-op movement is also. So we work hard building community spirit and connections. Each year, we celebrate International Co-operative Week with vigour. We have dances, family days, career days, and guest speakers. I'd say we have been successful. We've attracted new people, like Paul Gallant from Prince Edward Island, who is now the director of the Chéticamp Arts Council. He can do anything: teach, write musicals and plays, organize, direct. He came to Chéticamp because he saw the community was willing to work with him to develop his cultural projects. Le grand cercle has been the big hit of the Congrès, and without Paul, it never would have happened. The role of the Co-operative Council at home is to do everything we can to make sure the co-operative movement continues to grow and prosper. I'm not Paul, but I like to think a little bit of his success is also the success of the council.

The Women's Summit is open to Acadian and Francophone women and we will continue to work after the Congrès is over. We don't get much attention in the press, but that's okay. After the concerts and parties are all over, we will still be working away. In the end, I think that persistence pays off. We will continue to change things for Acadian women.

RUTH BLANCHARD, PIERRE PORT, LOUISIANA

Cynthia [Holland] and I first came to Canada for the 1994 Congrès. We had been part of a theatre group that created a play called Port Lajoie, which toured and played at the International Festival in Lafayette. We brought it up here for the first Congrès to show Acadian women and to see for the first time the country of our ancestors.

CYNTHIA HOLLAND, PIERRE PORT, LOUISIANA

We have been traveling around. In Chéticamp, we cooked for the cast of Le grand cercle: jambalaya, gumbo, and crawfish pie, and I tried some new dishes using some of our recipes but using northern ingredients: lobster, snow crab, shrimp. We're amateur cooks. We brought ingredients with us that would travel, like smoked and spiced sausage. We just do it for fun and it has been fun. We had a great time in that little kitchen, and met people from all over Canada.

ELAINE CLEMENT, LAFAYETTE, LOUISIANA

I came north for the first time seven years ago. I wanted to meet women from here before starting to organize in Louisiana. Our ancestors decided to leave Acadie but they didn't want to let their culture, language, or families fall apart. It's taken us a couple of centuries to start reconnecting our families between Louisiana and northern Acadie, but we're doing it now.

One of the first things I did was visit Grand-Pré. I wanted to see the Deportation Cross, the place where our ancestors were put on the ships. It's curious, but even though I'm Acadian and always knew my history, it wasn't until I was standing in front of that metal cross, looking out at the bay, that it really hit me what had happened. It isn't an easy thing to accept. I began to cry.

Liz Rignley dresses in period costume for a Live at 5 broadcast from the Grand-Pré historic site. The 2004 Congrès captured Canada's attention and was the centre of much local and national media coverage.

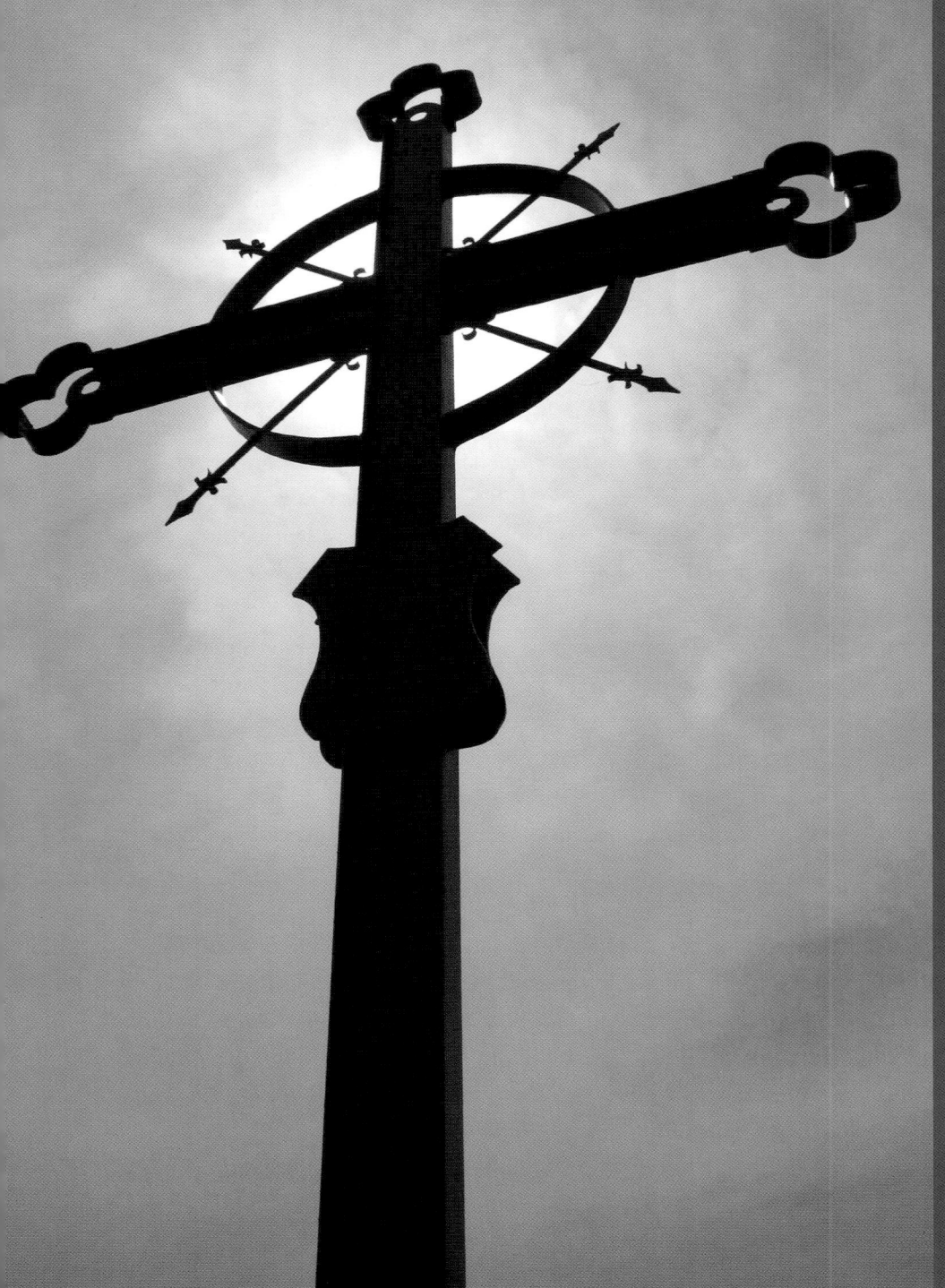

The sun shines behind the deportation cross at Grand-Pré. The cross was erected in 1924, two kilometres from the memorial church that was built on the site of the original Acadian parish of Saint-Charles-des-Mines.

ACADIAN SCHOOLS

FERNAND DOUCET (AUTHOR'S FATHER), GRAND ÉTANG

At sixteen, I was six feet tall and many people in the village didn't understand why I was still in school when I could have been out working, helping the family out. But my father was insistent that all his children go to school as long as possible, although it was very difficult. My sister Bernadette had to quit after grade eight to help out at home because our mother began to have serious problems with her legs. I know her lack of schooling remains a great regret for Bernadette to this day.

I had to take grade twelve at home. There was no teacher who could take me through the senior matriculation year. The priest helped me and so did my mother. I was very fortunate. Studies came easily to me, and in Grand Étang, we were fortunate to have a priest who was a gifted teacher in math, languages, and Latin. Without his and my parents' support, I wouldn't have made it. Any kind of education beyond the first few years was difficult, and if there was slightest little hitch, you had to quit. Today, to be honest, I find it astonishing how kids are nursed along. How many chances they get!

Chezzetcook is a small Acadian village of about two thousand souls at the head of an inlet of the Atlantic about thirty kilometres from Halifax. It was entirely French-speaking from its founding over two hundred years ago until the fifties, when the village school was consolidated, with the idea of giving the students the benefits of a larger school. In twenty years, the French language disappeared from village life. Chezzetcook has become a kind of watchword among Acadians for what happens when a village loses its Acadian school.

Sally Ross, co-author (with Alphonse Deveau) of *The Acadians of Nova Scotia*, is well known for her writing and Acadian scholarship. She taught at Dalhousie University for many years and is now an independent scholar and translator. We talked on the hillside at Grand-Pré.

Clive: Are you working on another book?

Sally: I have just finished a book called *Les écoles acadiennes en Nouvelle Écosse, 1758–2000* [Acadian Schools in Nova Scotia 1758–2000]. It's no wonder Acadians are so preoccupied with schools. The whole provincial school system was set up to assimilate Acadians into good British subjects. Acadians had to take exams in English. The curriculum was set up to minimize the French content.

Clive: Chéticamp seems to be doing well.

A stunning view of Cheticamp. This small fishing village was settled in the late 1700s by Acadians seeking a secure home after the Deportation. Saint-Pierre Church can be seen in the distance.

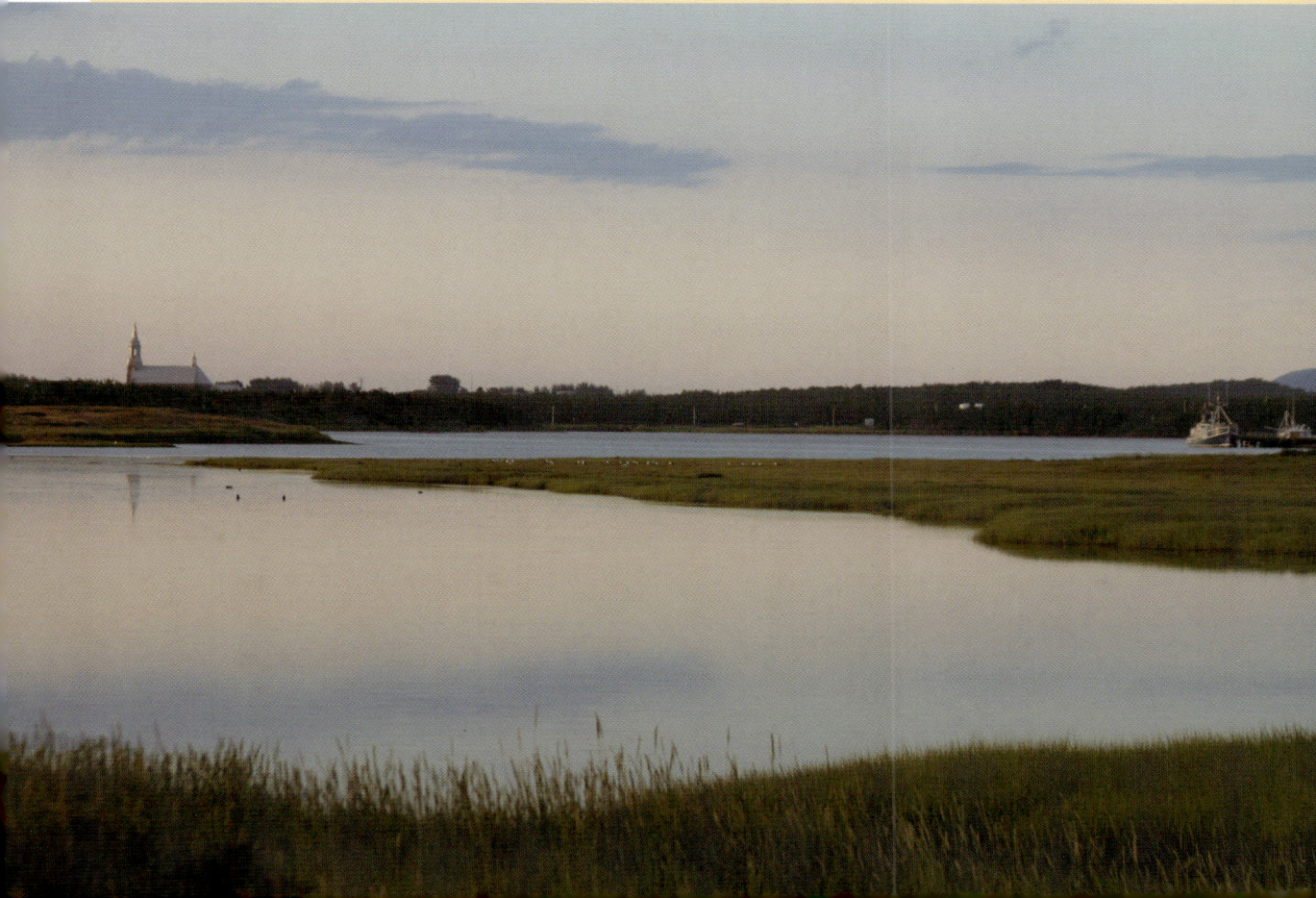

Sally: Chéticamp is one of the strongest. It has a French school now and the community, because of its isolation, has kept the language, but it's still very difficult. Of thirteen kids who will start school in Chéticamp this year, nine don't speak French at all. It's typical. English is the dominant language and when the culture is clearly dominated by one language, when you have mixed marriages, the children usually speak English at home. And now there is the added complication of a brand new English school in Belle Côte, nine kilometres away, which drains off students. Belle Côte used to be an entirely French-speaking village; it's now mostly English. It's hard no matter where you live.

Acadians are still taking the province to court to get French-language schools. Glenda Doucet in Baie Ste.-Marie just went all the way to the Supreme Court and got a favourable judgment, but it's not 1904 today, it's 2004. And she lives in a French-speaking region with no French-language school.

The bow of a tall ship standing in the Halifax harbour, with Georges Island in the background. Georges Island, a small drumlin with a long history as a prison site, is where many Acadians would have been held prisoner during the deportation.

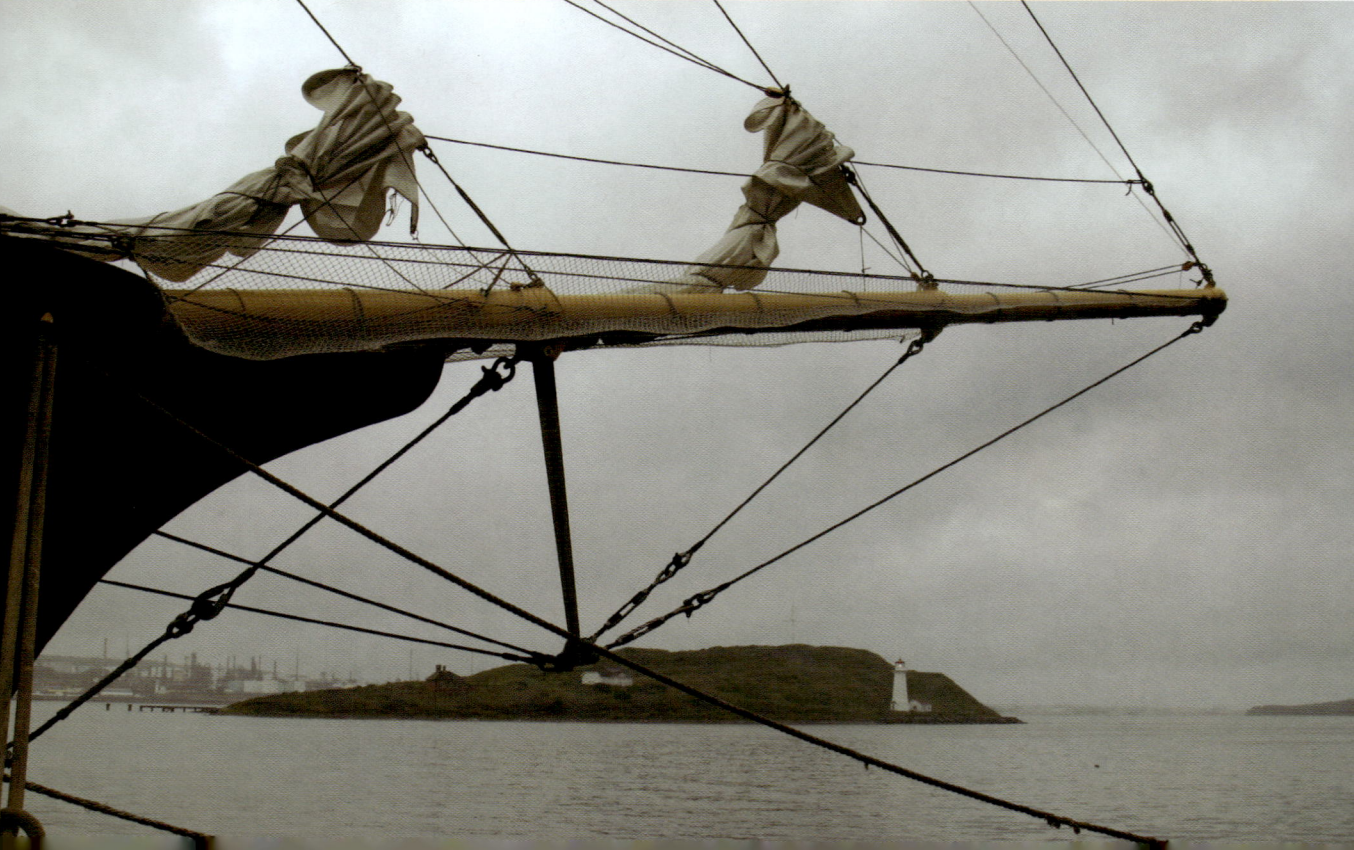

Chezzetcook always had a very strong French-language Acadian environment. French church, French in the stores, homes, and streets—but they got caught in a school consolidation. I don't think it was a deliberate policy on the part of the government; the school boards have been closing small schools for decades. There's hardly a village, town or city that hasn't been affected by it, but the effect on a village like Chezzetcook was to extinguish the language. Once they closed the village school down and bussed the kids to a consolidated English language school, that was it. It was an amazingly quick slide from French only to English only. I think the elders began to ask, "What is the point?" And the youngsters couldn't do much else but adapt. In the consolidated school, their numbers were just too small to maintain their own voices.

The history of Acadians in Nova Scotia is very different from that of New Brunswick. New Brunswick is shaped in a square, with all the Acadian communities in one corner of the square. Nova Scotia is shaped like an "L," and the Acadian communities are not in one region. Can you imagine how seldom people visited each other when it took two days to drive from Cape Breton to southern Nova Scotia? It still takes a full day.

Clive: How has the Congrès gone for you?

Sally: I've had a wonderful time. I've had a chance to visit with the Amiraults and Bourgeois at their family reunions. I'd like to thank all the organizers of the family reunions. It's no easy thing to organize a reunion for a thousand people!

CONVERSATION WITH DOUGLAS LAPIERRE, CHEZZETCOOK AND GATINEAU

[In 1755] my family was held prisoner in Halifax for a long time. There used to be a prison on Georges Island; now it is a tourist site. When I look at the island, I'm always struck by how small it is. How did they cram hundreds of men, women and children into it?

Part of my family was deported from there to North Carolina and then to France. The Bourgeois, Dugas, Breaux, Surettes, Trahans were all eventually sent south, but some were able to escape and found ways to stay. The Doucets, Bellefontaines, Cormiers—about ten families in all founded the village of Chezzetcook. We remained pretty much isolated and apart from Halifax, even though we were only thirty kilometres from the city until the 1960s. Then there was this kind of collapse. It was as if the whole village kind of turned its back on the past and the French language. Parents and grandparents refused to speak French to the children. The children were bussed outside of the village to go to school. The children themselves had no desire to learn French.

There was a lot of discrimination. I was a French teacher, and I can remember being told not to speak French in the teachers' lounge. It wasn't a Nova Scotian who told me, it was a South African who was ultimately fired, but I can feel the discrimination yet. An Acadian is fine as long as he isn't speaking French. I wanted my language to be more than a kitchen language. I left.

I'm here to celebrate the four hundredth anniversary of our ancestors' arrival and to be a translator for a delegation from France that is visiting our village. I'm happy to do it, but I find the visit sad.

Nova Scotia, not New Brunswick, is the birthplace of Acadie, and I want people to realize that. I'm also doing some genealogical research. I have relatives on the Magdalene Islands, in the Gaspé, and in Louisiana. We were spread all over the map. I want to know where all the different branches of the family ended up and who they were. We had a priest complete the genealogy of our village, but it is filled with errors. He denied or hid the relations with the Mi'kmaq. Bona Arsenault's books, which a lot of people quote, are also filled with errors for the same kinds of reasons. They hide our connections with the Mi'kmaw people.

My village is often forgotten, but that hasn't stopped me from celebrating. You have to celebrate when you can.

Allister Surette, president of the Congrés mondial acadien 2004, speaks at the official opening at Sainte-Anne University. Surette is a political and education activist committed to ensuring connectivity and growth in French education.

ALLISTER SURETTE, VICE-RECTEUR, UNIVERSITÉ SAINTE-ANNE AND PRESIDENT OF THE CMA

Alister Surette was the president of the Congrès mondial acadien 2004 and was present at all of the major events of the CMA—making speeches, welcoming people and generally acting as a link between the host communities of Nova Scotia and the thousands of visitors. As someone who has been a key figure both politically and on the education scene in Nova Scotia, his attention is focused on the problem of creating a sense of the Acadian community in a province where the Acadian villages are dispersed.

Allister: I grew up in the village of Argyle, which is at the end of the province. My education in the Acadian community started when I was elected and became Minister of Francophone and Acadian Affairs. The biggest problem for the Acadian community in Nova Scotia is that we are so dispersed. Until recently, I think many New Brunswick Acadians didn't even realize that there were any Acadians in Nova Scotia. For me, one of the biggest es is simply reminding people that we do still exist in the province

Nova Scotian Acadians themselves are often unaware of other communities in their own province and it's understandable. There was no easy way to communicate between the Baie Ste.-Marie region, Isle Madame, Chéticamp, and Halifax. The Acadian communities in these places remain more myth than reality for many people. I can't count the number of Acadians who have said to me, "Do they really still speak French in Argyle? Do they really still speak French in Isle Madame?" As if the only place the French language existed was in your own village among your own family. Modern communication is changing this lack of knowledge in a way that nothing else has. The radio stations in Baie Ste.-Marie, Isle Madame, and Chéticamp can now share programming. Our little college system, the Collège d'Acadie, can now serve every village and region of Nova Scotia using the internet. Our teachers can now have a classroom that extends through the air across hundreds of kilometres. People can send letters and information of all kinds to each other more easily and more cheaply than using the telephone. This has given us new capacity for self-development that has never existed before. The trick now is to find ways to use these new methods of communicating with each other in the best ways possible. That's what the Collège d'Acadie is all about.

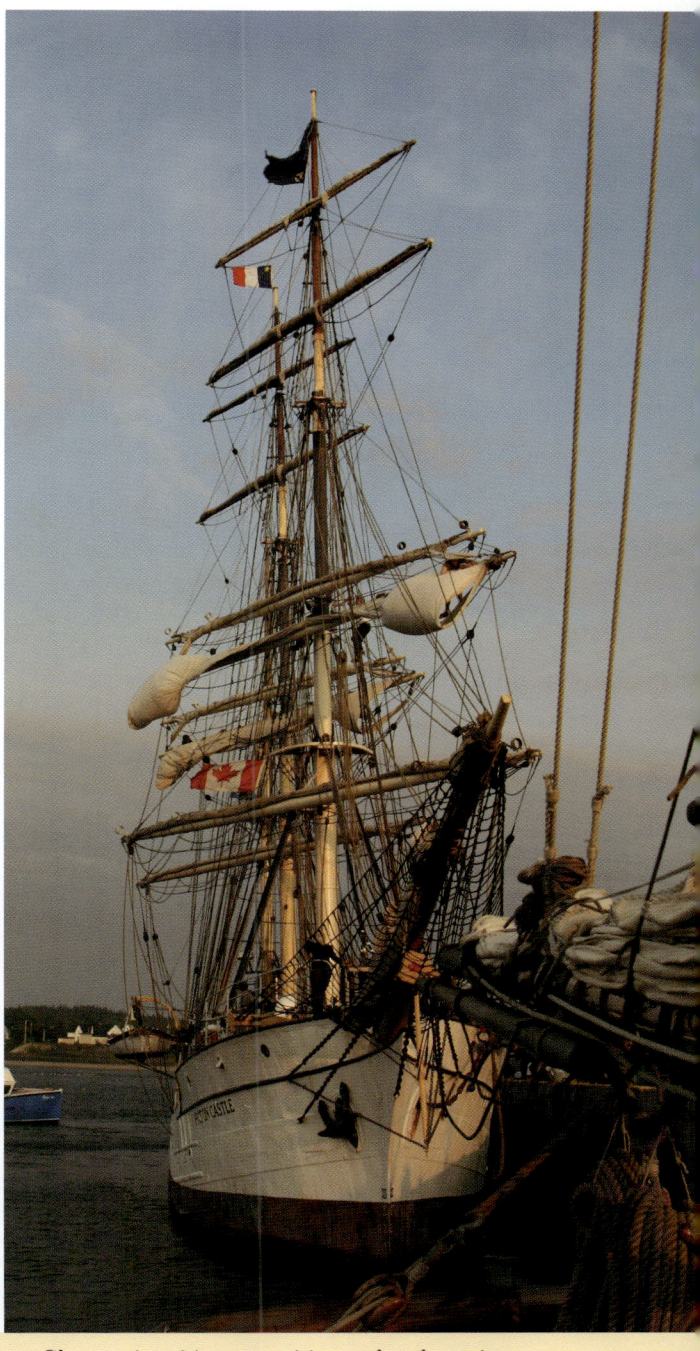

A perfect day for a sail! Tall ships arrive at the wharf in Methegan, Clare, to give visitors an exciting on-board experience.

9

CLOSING MASS, GRAND-PRÉ

Ave Maris stella
Dei Mater alma
Atque semper Virgo
Felix coeli porta

– Acadian National Anthem, from Découvrir l'Acadie, Le Courrier de Nouvelle Ecosse

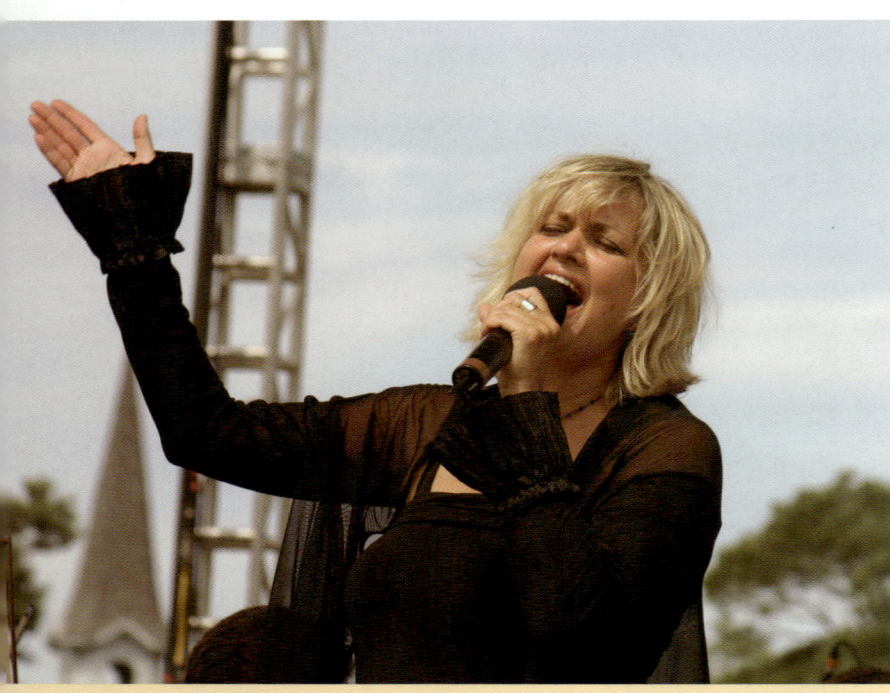

Instead of trying to find a parking spot near Grand-Pré for the closing mass, we decided to park in the town of Wolfville six kilometres from Grand-Pré and then bicycle along the old Acadian dykes back towards Grand-Pré. The traffic into Grand-Pré was dense, but once we passed the village, the road became clear. The morning was sparkling, the sky clear—a perfect day for an outdoor mass.

Lina Boudreau sings Ave Maria, an unofficial anthem of the Acadians, backed up by Symphony Nova Scotia.

It was easy to find the dyke. It swings right into the edge of the town and there is a parking lot right next to it. We took our bicycles off the car and without further ado began to cycle along the flat top of the dyke. On one side of the dyke, there are fields of corn stretching to the horizon; on the other, wild grasses and red muddy flats of the Bay of Fundy. The top of the dyke is strewn with wildflowers and points directly towards the distant majesty of Cape Blomidon. This is not a wild landscape. There is a feeling of serenity here.

Grand-Pré means "great field," and the view from the dykes gives a powerful impression of what a vast and fruitful field it still is. The spire of the church at Grand-Pré is the only encumbrance the eye meets in the sweep of land and sea and sky. You can see why the Mi'kmaq gave their creator-magician Glooscap his home at Cape Blomidon. This great rocky promontory has the feel of the infinite.

The sense of pilgrimage is strong as thousands gather for a high mass. This solemn, majestic, and classic event speaks to the spiritual roots of Acadian traditions, bringing Acadian cousins together from all over the world.

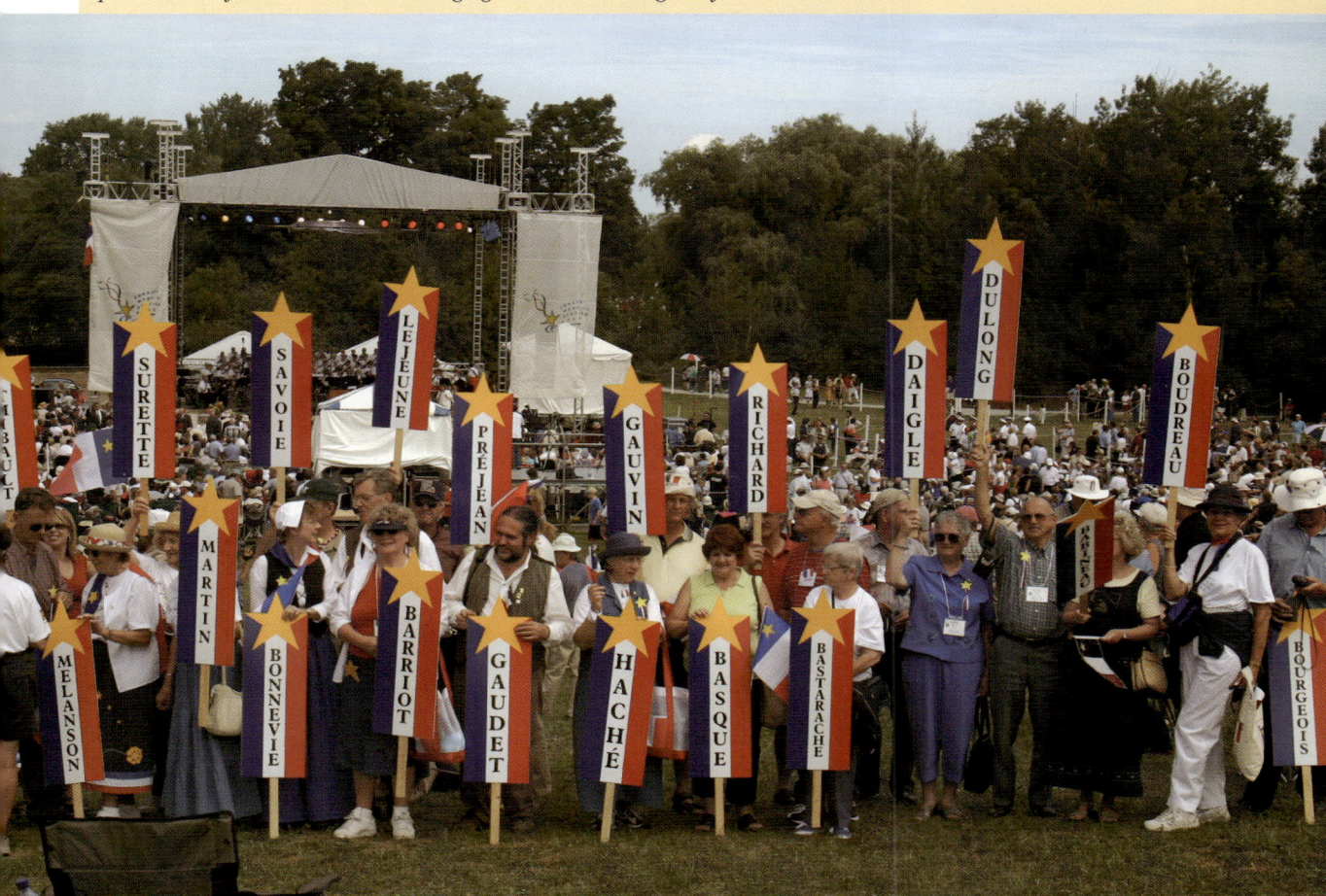

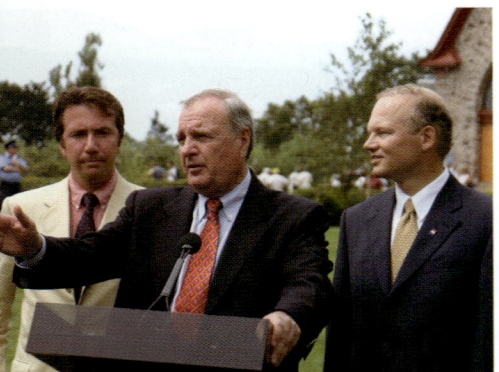

Canadian Prime Minister Paul Martin stands with other government representatives in front of the church at Grand-Pré. The Canadian government was a proud supporter of the 2004 Acadian Congrès.

The dyke veers out into the bay, away from the modern village of Grand-Pré, and creates a magnificent spoon of land in front of the church. But if we had stayed with the path and the dyke, it would have taken us far away from the village, so we rode our bicycles down from the height of the dykes onto one of the farmers' roads that cut over the fields. The church spire in the distance oriented us and we made our way towards it.

The media was gathered in front of the Interpretation Centre, waiting for the Prime Minister and other notables to arrive. I watched the crowd flowing by. It was a festive gathering rather than a pious one. There were no suits, no white shirts and ties, no sombre faces. Acadian flags were printed on everyone and everything that moved. There were Acadian headscarves, neckscarves, hats, big flags, small flags, carry bags with flags, red and white flashing buttons, vests, dresses, face paint, and T-shirts, T-shirts, T-shirts. It was as if we want to tattoo our acadienité right onto our bodies so that no one could mistake us for anything else, not even for a second.

On the hillside, thousands waited for the mass to begin. The assembled dignitaries on the stage—like the Prime Minister, the Mi'kmaw Grand Chief, and the Bishop of Halifax—were just dots.

The mass began. It was a grand spectacle, with choirs and speakers, and the dignitaries were many: in attendance were Keptin Frank Nevin, District Chief of the Mi'kmaq Nation; Michel Cyr, president of the Société nationale de l'Acadie; Benoit Pelletier of Quebec, Minister of Intergovernmental and Indian Affairs; and Clara Baudoin, Louisana State Representative.

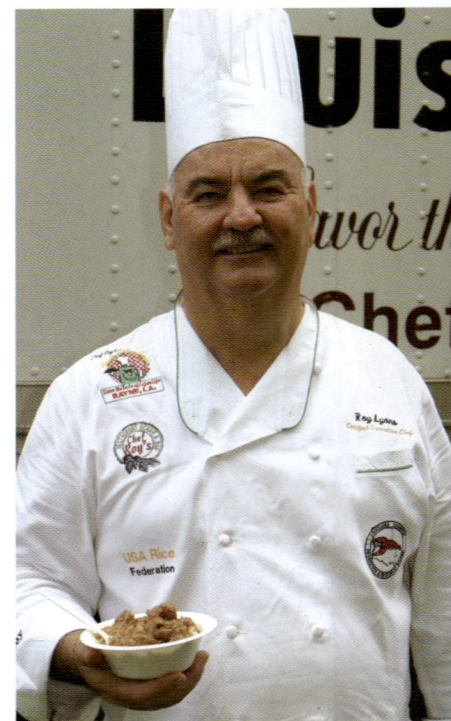

The famous Chef Roy towed his massive eighteen-wheeler kitchen all the way from Louisiana! His efforts didn't get wasted: the crowds were delighted with the incredible tastes of authentic Cajun gumbo and jambalaya.

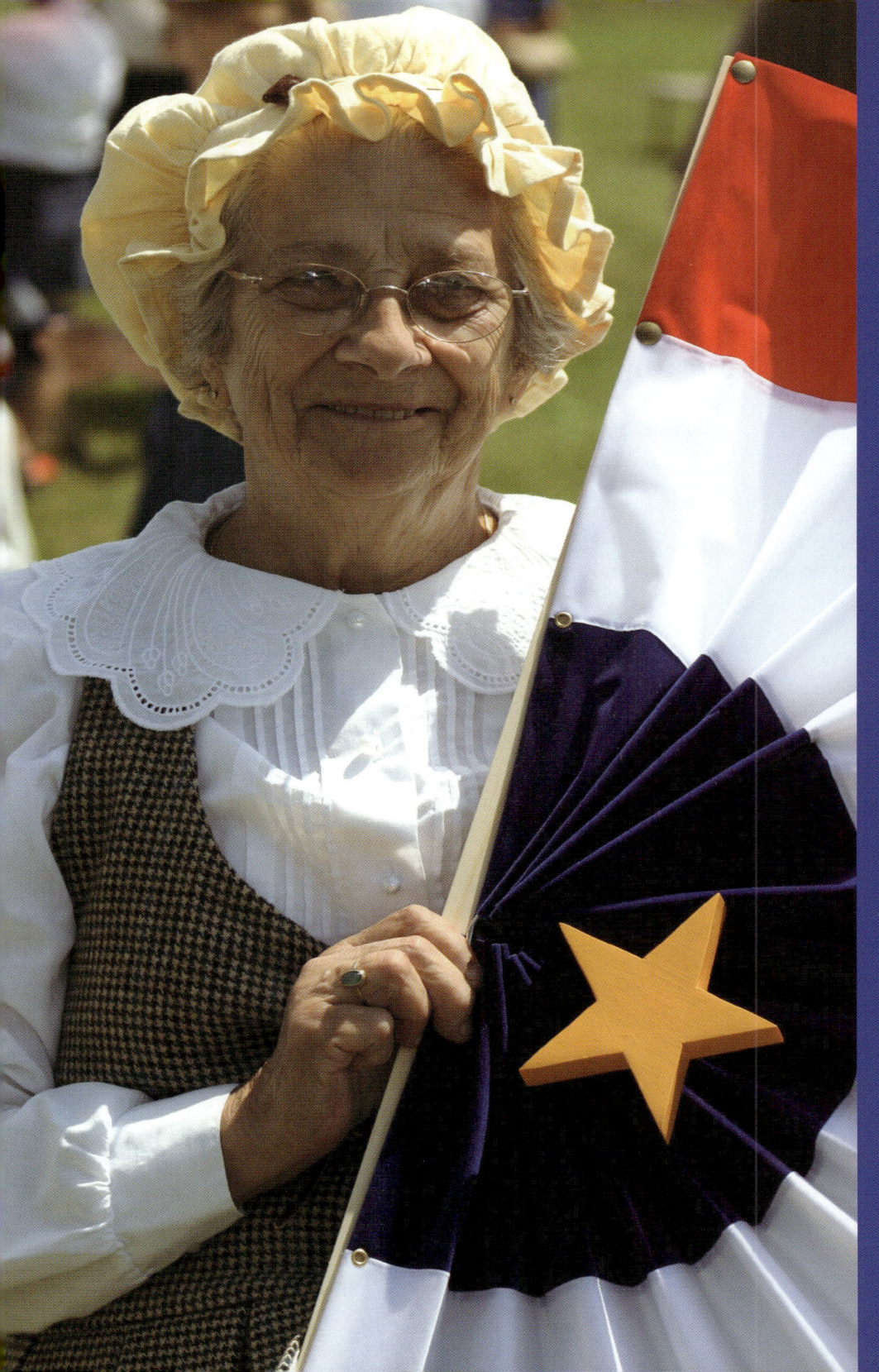

Acadian Marie D'Eon displays her handmade Acadian flag. She follows a proud tradition: The first flag was sewn by Marie Babineau, and remains on display at the Acadien Museum at Moncton University. The flag, designed by Father Marcel–François Richard, was adopted in 1884 at the second Acadian Congrès at Mischouche, PEI.

At the back of the stage were an orchestra and three choirs: two from Nova Scotia and one from St. Martinville, Louisiana. The closing mass was entirely different from the opening one, which was subdued and serious. The crowd at the closing mass was respectful and quiet, but there was an electric, joyful current that seemed to vibrate through everyone there. The stage was large, but there were so many people on it that it looked like an overcrowded boat about to sink.

Directly behind the stage was a canopy of green trees broken only by the spire of the memorial church. It made a grand and vibrant scene, the thousands of people massed on the hillside and the red, white and blue colours with the star of Acadie everywhere you looked. And the thought came to me again that it was incredible we were there, at the exact place our ancestors were taken from everything that they knew and marched down to the sea at bayonet point, many never to see their loved ones again, the boys refusing to be separated from their fathers, the women's cries of disbelief. How pleased they would be to see us all here on the hillside, remembering them, keeping faith with them—the Leblancs and the Beliveaus, the Amiraults and the Melansons and the Comeaus, all at Grand-Pré together.

CONVERSATION WITH CYPRIEN OKANA, MONCTON

I noticed two children—who, unlike the vast majority of Congrès attendees, were not white—playing near me on the day of the closing mass, and went to speak to their father, Cyprien Okana from Zaire. He came to the Université de Moncton to study in the 1980s, married a Leblanc, and stayed.

Cyprien: I'm a marketing consultant. The Congrès is a good thing, very well-organized. It's the second one that I've attended. But I have the impression sometimes that the Acadians are a people trapped in their past, who have difficulty in opening up to strangers.

I have suffered misery, famine, humiliation, but it never affected my morale. The Acadians have suffered in the same way. It was really the native people who got them through it. It seems to me the Acadians should be a kind of light for all minorities, both in how to survive and how to welcome people into their house.

Clive: But we do. You are married to a Leblanc, and when I saw your children playing on the hillside, I thought: "There is the future of Acadie." That's why I came to talk to you.

Cyprien: I see what you mean. I guess what is bothering me is that these last weeks, all I have heard on the radio is, "I am a Richard," "I am a Landry," "I am a Bastarache," as if the only way you can be an Acadian is to have one of these names. My children will be Okana, but they might consider themselves to be Acadian also.

Clive: I hope they do.

As I was leaving Grand-Pré, a journalist from Quebec stopped me. Pointing towards the fields stretching towards Cape Blomidon, he asked me: "Did you think that these world gatherings will eventually lead to Acadians asking for their land back?" I replied: "You don't understand. Acadian history is more complicated than the history of Quebec. We had no cannon and no stone walls. We weren't trying to conquer anyone. The English were *nos amis, les ennemis*. The Mi'kmaq were *nos voisins*. We built our *aboiteaux* here. This is the place our ancestors are buried. This is the place they created the bountiful fields and orchards that they loved and we remember today. There is not one Acadian song about missing France or wanting revenge. There are hundreds of songs about the Acadie our ancestors loved yet refused to kill people for. We honour their spirits by coming here. This is a holy place for us. You occupy a holy place with your spirit."

Susan Knutson, arrayed in traditional Acadian costume for Evangeline, the musical drama presented by Araignées du bouiboui, at Sainte-Anne University. The story of Evangeline, based on H. W. Longfellow's epic poem of the same name written in 1847, continues to be a source of inspiration for the Acadian people.

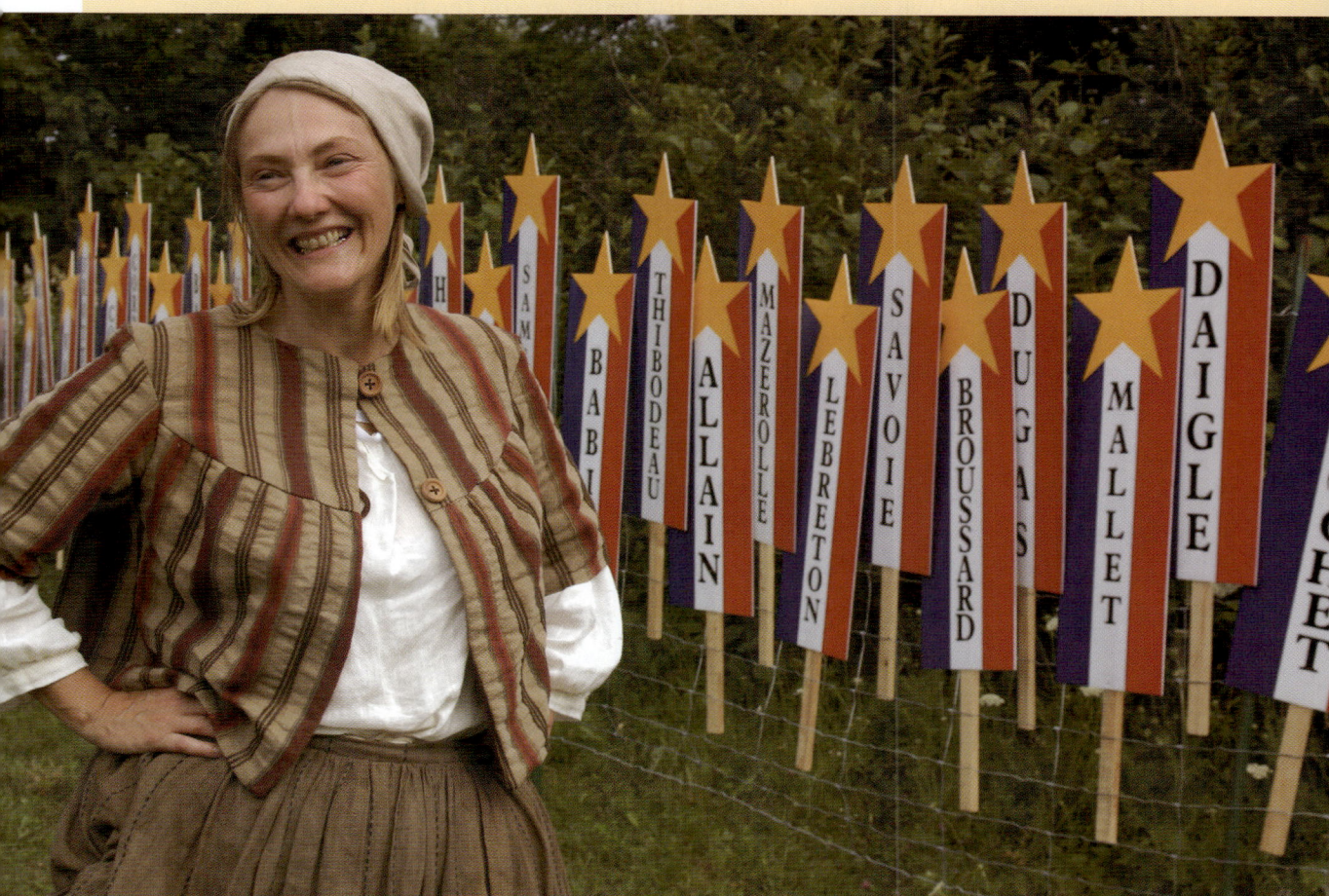

10

CLOSING CONCERT, CITADEL HILL

Reveil! Reveil! Wake-up! Wake-up!

The concert stage was at the bottom of Citadel Hill. There was a flat space in front of it, enough space for several thousand people, but the bulk of the audience camped out on the steep hillside in tightly packed rows. We sat just above the flat grassy area on the first rise, so we had an unobstructed view of the stage; behind and above us was a great sea of people and flags and joyous rustle.

Some people arrived at four in the afternoon, even though the concert didn't start until nine o'clock. We joined in the tintamarre [parade] at six o'clock and came to the hill straight afterward, but time didn't seem to matter. There was visiting and talking to be done.

Inside the gates, we joined up with Douglas Lapierre from Chezzetcook, a school teacher now living in Gatineau, Quebec. We had met earlier in the Congrès and had talked about the history of his family and village. He was also in the tintamarre, a celebratory parade. He was shocked at my attire—the only Acadian paraphenalia I wore was my Grand-Pré cap. Douglas wore an Acadian flag as a cape, an Acadian headband, and face paint, and he carried clappers. I just banged on my notebook and yelled "Vive l'Acadie!" Not good enough. He loaned me his clappers and Patty, my wife, passed me a flag. The evening was mild and warm. We settled in to watch the gathering crowd and talk.

Douglas Lapierre: I went to Chezzetcook kind of upset, feeling like the token Acadien who still spoke French for this delegation from France. I feel differently now. It was an amazing experience. I have never seen so much pride in our village, genuine pride. It wasn't attached to anything in particular. How could it be? All the big celebrations are going on in the villages where they have kept the language, but it was as if a big wall had come tumbling down. People were unafraid to say they were Acadian, to think they were Acadian, to express themselves as

Acadians. I've never seen that before in Chezzetcook. I was so proud of my village. You know where it comes from? It comes from genealogy. The young people began to see that the names on the genealogical trees in the prison in Halifax Harbour, in the Magdalen Islands, in Louisiana, and in New Brunswick were more than just names on paper; they were once real, breathing humans who had stood in their shoes just like we do today. I had this really strong vision that our young people have finally realized what their ancestors had gone through, and that they had never, ever given up; instead of feeling ashamed of them, the young people felt proud. I have never seen this before in Chezzetcook.

A giant tintamarre showcases some of the best masks, costumes and grosse têtes made by Acadian artisans. Centred around the theme 1604–2004, the figures within the Citadel Parade celebrate Acadian heroes. Douglas Lapierre holds the flag.

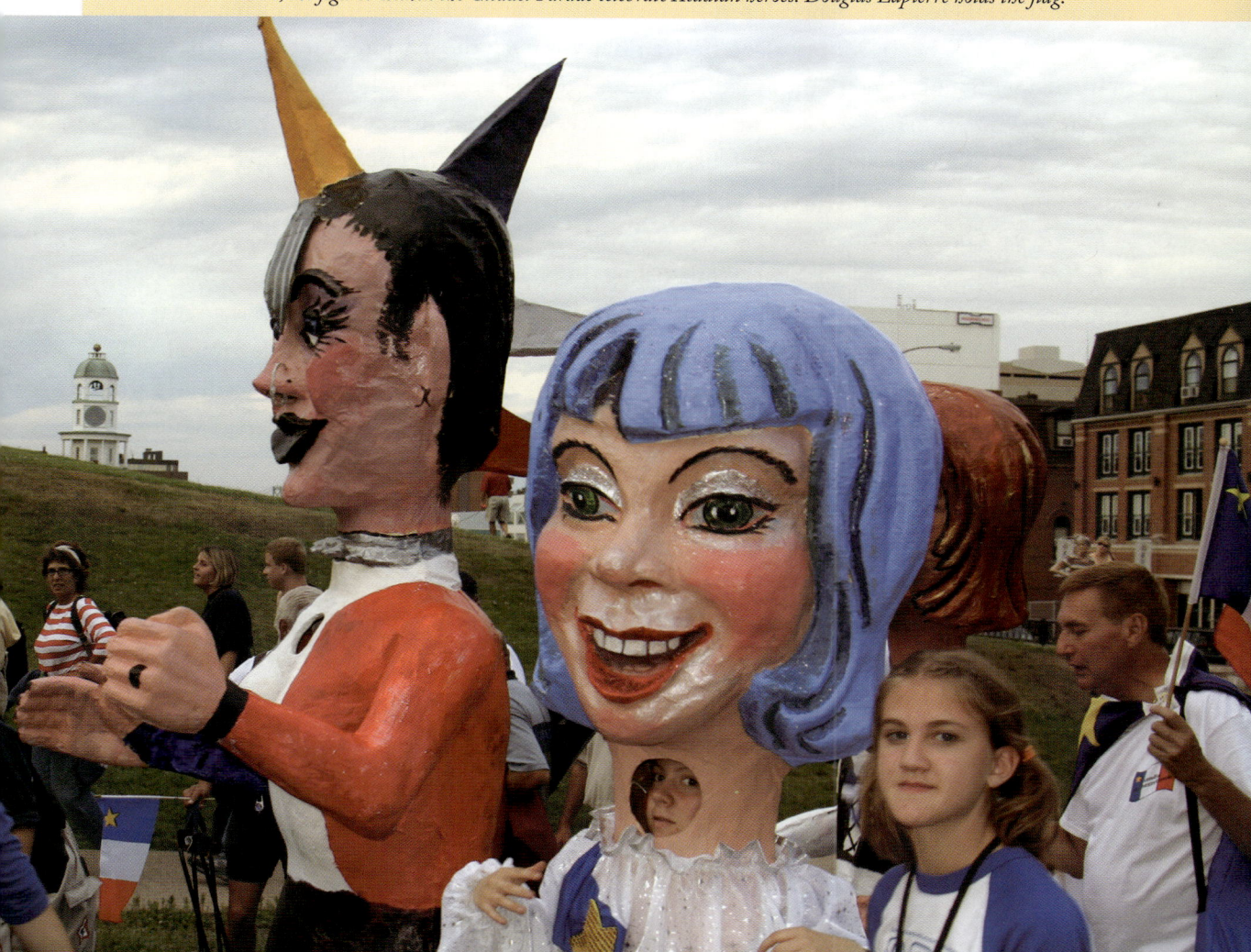

CONVERSATIONS WITH JEANNE GIONET, DELPHINE GIONET BERGERON, PAT GIONET CARRIERE

On the hillside, I was sitting, by chance, with three retired women now living in Montreal and Quebec City, though they were all originally from Caraquet. What follows are some snippets of conversation from that evening on the hillside in which they talked about each other, their lives, and why they came to the Congrès.

Jeanne Gionet: I'm from Montreal. I'm divorced. This trip is putting me in the red but I don't care. I had to come. It was impossible to resist. Our artists are so impressive. It makes me proud to hear them. I wish my parents could be here. They showed us how to be happy with very little and how to fit in—no matter where. I see this around us here. Look how clean the grounds are. People take the time to put their bottles in the garbage cans. I like that people care about where they are. Even here in this English fort—which, when you think about it, isn't such a great place for an Acadian to be. In Montreal, on St. Jean Baptiste Day, the day after the fête the parks are so littered with junk, it takes the city the entire day to clean them up. I don't like that.

Delphine Gionet Bergeron: Does anyone want a beer? I'm going to the beer tent. Ouch, my legs are creaky! [Before she goes I ask her why she is here.] To meet people. For friendship. To express my solidarity with others. To laugh.

Pat Gionet Carriere: And to learn.

Jeanne: I have never visited Nova Scotia before. I was never conscious that there were Acadians on Cape Breton Island. I always thought that Acadie was just New Brunswick. It is a great joy to see all the flags and the enthusiasm. When I was young it felt like we were a little group lost in the woods. People made fun of our accents. It used to be a shameful thing to be Acadian. I would not admit it to anyone easily. Now it is a glory. What a change. That's why I'm here; I want to be part of that change.

Pat: I live in Quebec City now, but I'm from Caraquet. It was a very hard decision to come because I always take my holidays in Caraquet and I have a big family there. But I thought, it's time I went to Nova Scotia, just to see what the place is like. I'm glad that I did. It is a beautiful province, but like Jeanne said, the thing that most impresses me is our enthusiasm to celebrate. It is as if people have been waiting to dance, like we've never done it before. Have you ever seen anything like it?

I come from a family of twelve; Delphine [she nods in the direction of Delphine, who is rapidly disappearing into the crowd in search of beer] is from a family of fifteen. Such large families seem strange now, but our mothers married very young, eighteen or nineteen, and there was no birth control, no pill. By the time you were thirty, you could easily have six or seven children about your skirts. You should talk with Delphine. She was the oldest and she helped raise her mother's family and then had three of her own. She is an amazing woman. She taught me in school and was the reason I became a school teacher.

In our time, we had no telephone, no television. We memorized poems. Delphine has the memory of an elephant. She has memorized *Evangeline* and when we are on the bus, she recites poetry for us. She knows all the villages of Acadie. She's been to Pubnico and Baie Ste.-Marie before. It's all new to me. I can't keep the names of the villages straight.

Delphine has traveled all over the world but her parents never left Caraquet. Delphine's father was a good fisherman, but in those days, you got pennies for a boatload of fish. Sometimes it was hardly worth selling them. Her family did well. There are three nurses in her family and a priest.

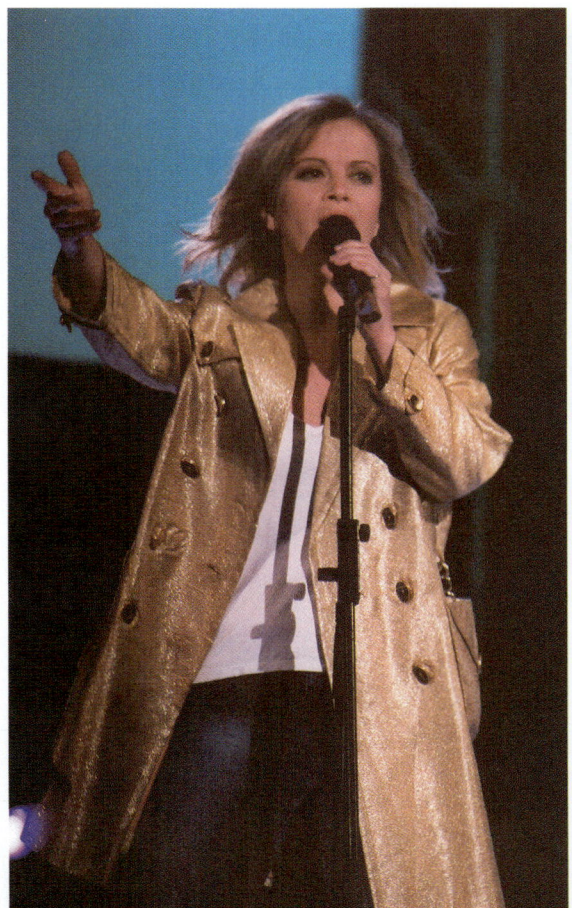
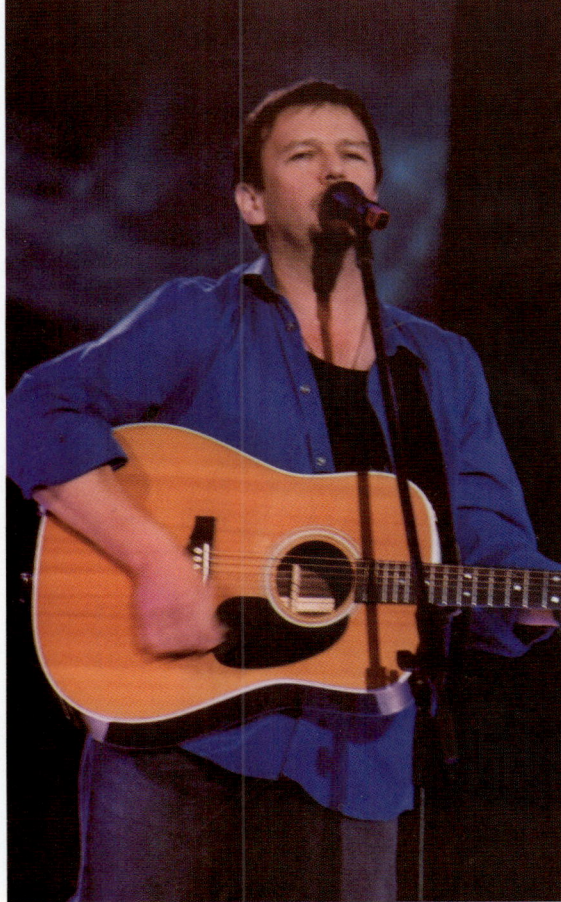

Isabelle Roy and Lennie Gallant sing their hearts out at the closing concert.

She pushed them all to learn. She loves to learn. She travels simply to learn about other places. She writes well in French and in English. How many people can do that?

Jeanne: You are a fan.

Pat: I am. She is eighty-one. She is the oldest woman among us and who entertains us the most on the bus? Delphine. Who remembers everything? Delphine. Who has more joie de vivre?

Clive: What about you? What did you do?

Pat: I was a school teacher. I taught little canayens.

Clive: May I ask how old you are?

Pat: I'll soon be 73.

Patrice Boulianne, the lead singer of Blou, stood not far from the crowd in front of a single microphone. Behind him were three young girls in Breton skirts and hats carrying Acadian flags. Suddenly the lights onstage dimmed, and the hillside was plunged into the twilight of a summer evening. Patrice stepped up to the microphone and called out into the night the single haunting word that starts Zachary Richard's great song "Reveil!"

The word "Reveil!" echoed and then faded away. Nothing more but emptiness and silence.

The lights came up on the stage, and in the centre was Zachary Richard himself, running to the microphone. "Reveil! Reveil! Reveil!" he thundered. This time the word was not hesitant, lonely, or fading. His call was insistent, repeated, strong; the words thrilled and tore though the night air. The great crowd scrambled to its feet, cheering, flags waving. The concert had begun.

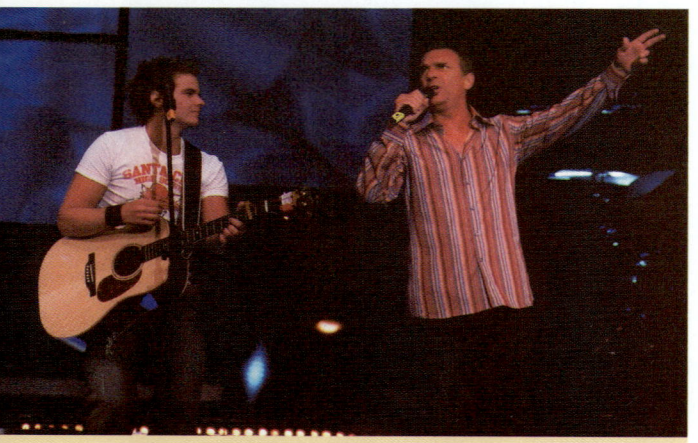

Zachary Richard, right, performs with Wilfred Lebouthillier at the closing concert, Citadel Hill.

All the performers conveyed a sense of community. They shared each other's songs, and you could feel the respect that they gave the doyens of Acadian song—Edith Butler and Zachary Richard. They anchored the show with confidence and energy like two great masts about which the rest of the cast sails.

Behind the electronic wall on the grass, one dancer in particular caught my eye: a young man who moved with great fluidity and rock-solid timing. He danced a very fast foxtrot; I've seen exactly the same dance in Louisiana. His partner couldn't really keep up with him, but his step was so smooth and assured all

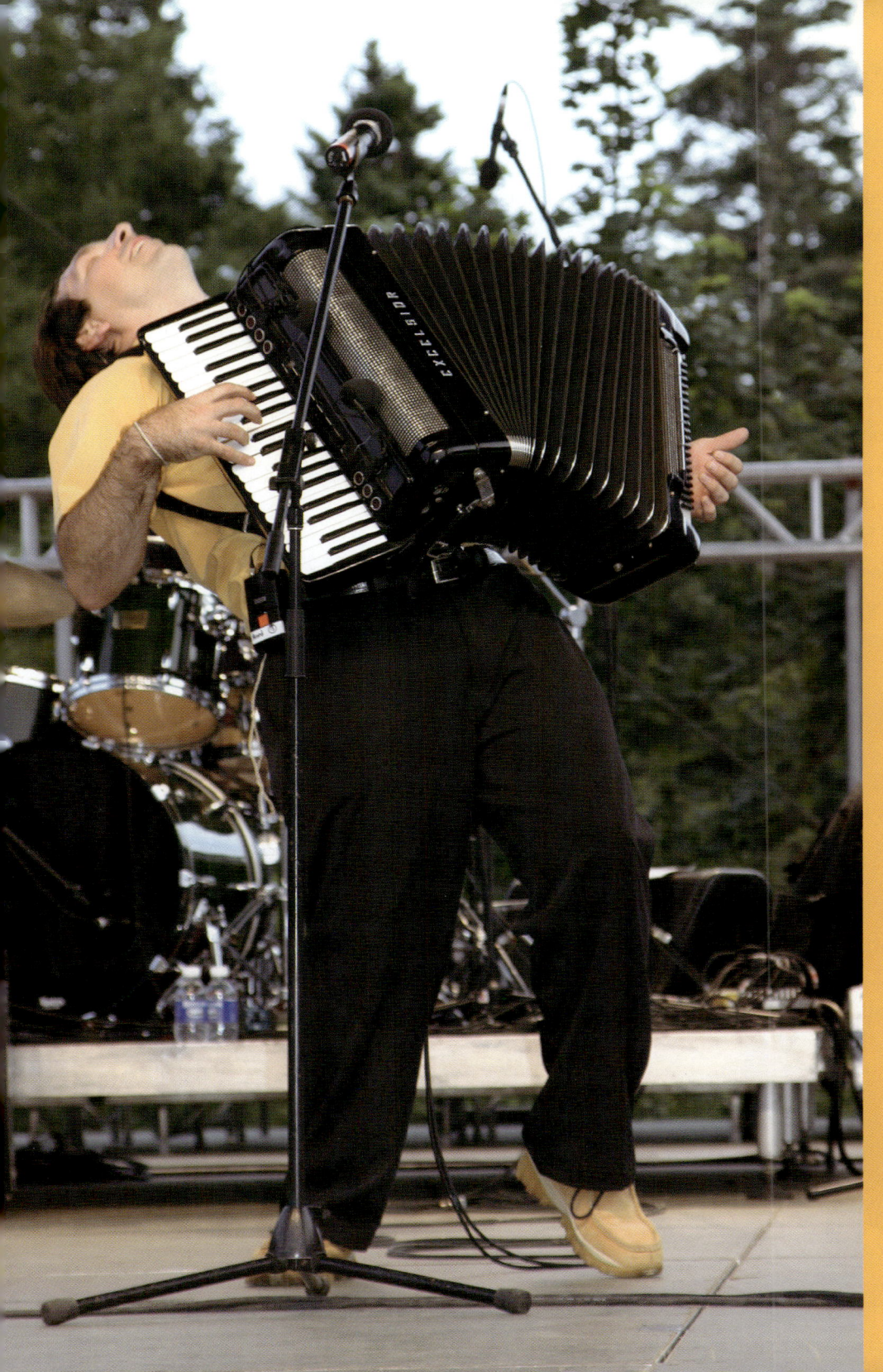

Patrice Boulianne from the group Blou belts out an Acadian tune. Of Franco-Manitoban origin, Boulianne founded the upbeat group with Len Leblanc and Daniel Leblanc of Nova Scotia. The popular group has achieved numerous awards, such as a 1999 East Coast Music Award for Francophone Recording of the Year.

she really had to do is hang onto his arms. When the dance ended I approached him. I began speaking in French, but he replied, "I can't speak French." There was a Surette name tag on his shirt, blinking with red, white, and blue lights.

I switched to English, explaining that I was writing a book on the Congrès and would like a few words with him. I was positive from his dancing and his cowboy boots that he was a Louisiana Cajun, but I learned once again not to jump to conclusions.

Clive: Where did you learn to dance like that?

Monsieur Surette: In Ontario.

Clive: Are you from Ontario?

Monsieur Surette: Yes, Cannington, but my father is a Surette from Wedgeport. I am the son of Wayne, who is the son of Kenneth.

Clive: What brings you to the Congrès?

Monsieur Surette: My sister is getting married and I needed to come back to Canada to put my emigration papers together for Australia.

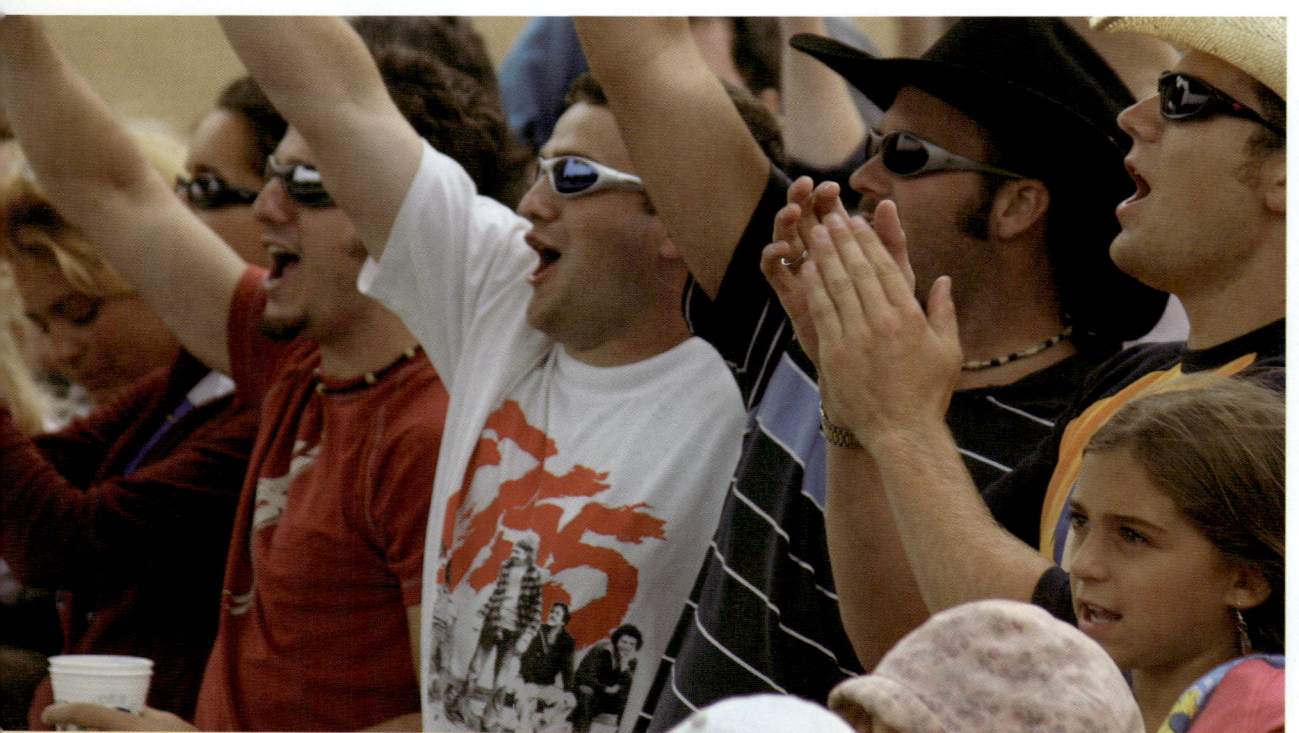

Enthusiastic fans of the popular Acadian group 1755 shout their appreciation during an outdoor concert in Clare.

Clive: Ever been to Louisiana?

Monsieur Surette: Nope.

Clive: They dance just like you do in Louisiana.

Monsieur Surette: I've been told that but I've never been to Louisiana. I just taught myself.

We shook hands, and I headed back to the hillside while Monsieur Surette headed back to the grassy dance floor.

Song followed song. Le Grand Dérangement tore up the stage with their dancing and fiddling. Singers and musicians from every corner of Acadie thundered, wailed, crooned from the stage in one powerful tune after another. Edith Butler sang alone with only the beat of her foot for accompaniment. It is the hardest way to sing, yet her magnificent voice carried it off.

It was not just the people of Acadie that were reunited, from Louisiana to Prince Edward Island; hundreds of years of musical tradition, from folk songs to the hip hop of Jacobus and Maleco, also joined, to become twenty-first century fusion music. There were African rhythms, Old World French melodies, North American rock and blues, Acadico/Zydeco. All these musical traditions have been wrapped up in the music of one very small, very scattered people.

As the last words of the last song roared out from the entire cast, the heavens opened up and rain descended in torrents from the night sky. The last concert on the last night of the last day was over. The rain was warm and welcome. We ran back through the streets of Halifax towards the waterfront and our hotel, soaked and exuberant. Four hundred years in the life of the Acadian people in North America had now been officially celebrated.

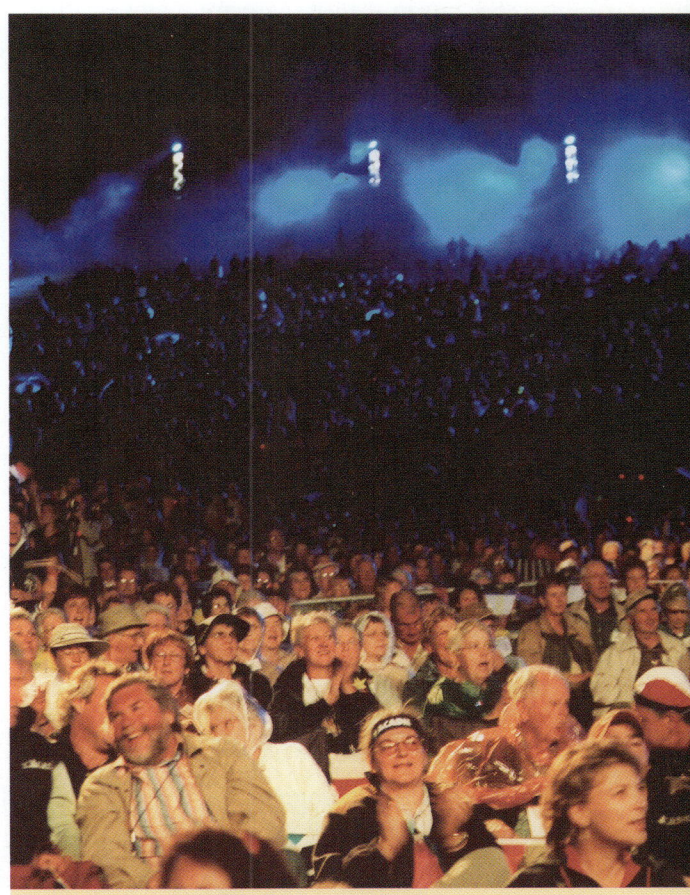

An exuberant crowd at the closing concert.

11

HIGHLIGHTS FROM THE FAMILY REUNIONS

Ave Maris Stella was chosen as the Acadian national anthem at Miscouche, Prince Edward Island in 1884, but in reality there are many Acadian anthems. Each family has a song. The Women's Summit and the Youth Assembly had theme songs commissioned for their gatherings. Many Acadians would choose *Reveil* by Zachary Richard as the anthem of the twenty-first century. Others would choose a song by Edith Butler or Donat Lacroix. Acadie has a great library and it is filled with music—soaring melodies, jigs, reels, waltzes, foxtrots, complaints, songs of loss and love, happy memory and an imagined future. Here is the first verse and refrain of the Gaudet family song, composed by Ernest F. Gaudet.

We are the children, descendants
Of the Gaudet family
Whose roots began long ago
In the heart of old France
The line has expanded and established
Itself in the land of Acadie
With pride and courage, its children
Have gone forward and flourished.

Oh yes, we are the Gaudets.

During the 2004 Congrès, over a hundred family reunions took place across Nova Scotia in schools, fire halls, universities, and community gathering places of all kinds. Although each reunion had its own unique flavour, there were many elements that were common to all. A family mass often opened the reunions. There were visits to historic sites, family songs, evening concerts, lectures on Acadian history and genealogy, craft and book sales, buttons and T-shirts, dancing, a lot of hugging, and food, food, food. But each family gave its own unique twist to their gathering. The Amiraults, for example, are enlisting DNA research in the quest to complete their genealogical story.

THE AMIRAULT FAMILY REUNION, WEST PUBNICO, AUGUST 8, 2004

By Ina Amirault

The quest for family ties and the strengthening of family bonds were the underlying themes of the gathering of the descendants of François Amirault dit Tourangeau and Marie Pitre, married around 1683.

It was a beautiful Sunday in West Pubnico when 750 people took part in the reunion activities. This was a return visit to Pubnico for many, but an emotional first trip to Nova Scotia and the cradle of Acadie for others.

They answered the irresistible call to come home from New England, California, Oklahoma, Yukon, Ontario, Quebec, Nova Scotia, and elsewhere. The different spellings of the family name were astonishing—Amirault, Amero, Amiro are common in Nova Scotia, but there were also Mireault, Amireault, Mero, Emero, Mirault and Merrow.

The usual accoutrements for family reunions were available—name tags, lapel pins, family pictures, genealogical research,

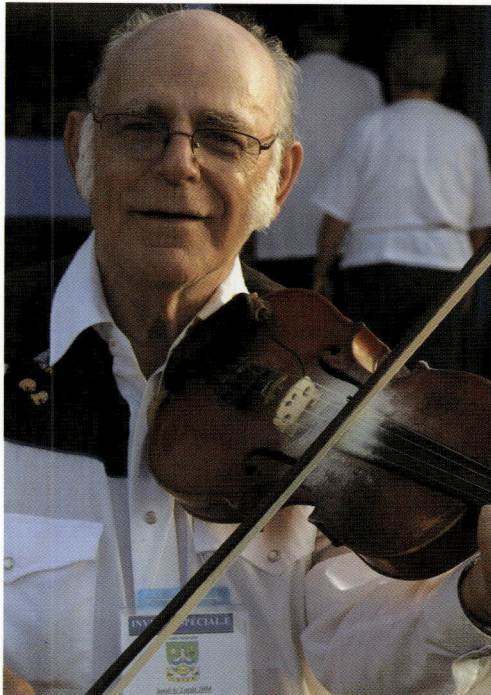

"Bayo" Everett Thibodeau is a legendary fiddler from Saint Mary's Bay. As a special guest at the Gaudet family reunion, Bayo's toe-tapping fiddle tunes evoked the Acadian musical heritage that remains strong in the community.

refreshments, kids' activities, and hand-made crafts to buy. The music and dancing started right after lunch and went on into the early morning the next day as talented family members and friends entertained.

Science played a part in this reunion, too, with the unveiling of an Amirault DNA project. Using "Y" chromosome DNA testing, the Amirault family hopes to find the missing pieces of the family puzzle.

The family's oldest known ancestor was said to be a Tourangeau, so he likely came from the Touraine province of France, or so one would think. Unfortunately, no records have been found to confirm where he came from, how or why he came to Acadie, or who he left behind.

Given the fact that certain parts of the "Y" chromosome remain unchanged through generations of male descendants, DNA testing could identify a relationship between a known descendant of François Amirault in North America and an Amirault still living in France. Once a match is found, a study of the Frenchman's ancestors might produce leads useful in identifying François Amirault dit Tourangeau.

So far, the DNA of seven living North American male descendants of two of François' sons has been tested and they are an exact match—they have the same haplotype. Eight living men in France with the family name Amirault or a variation were also tested. To the surprise of all, they don't match the North American men, and in most cases, they don't even match each other! Test results show six different haplotypes within the eight Frenchmen tested. The project will continue.

At the end of the day, tired Amirault family members exchanged hugs and kisses, email addresses, and genealogies. DNA research will help complete their family tree, but not today.

THE MIUS/MUISE/MEUSE FAMILY REUNION, BELLEVILLE, AUGUST 7, 2004

By Evelyn Muise

L'Association des Mius (Muise, Meuse) de la Nouvelle-Écosse held their family reunion at École Belleville. Over six hundred members attended the reunion, to the satisfaction of all the organizers. By all accounts, those in attendance had a wonderful time listening to speakers, examining photos, finding old, forgotten, and even new relatives, chatting with long lost friends and neighbours,

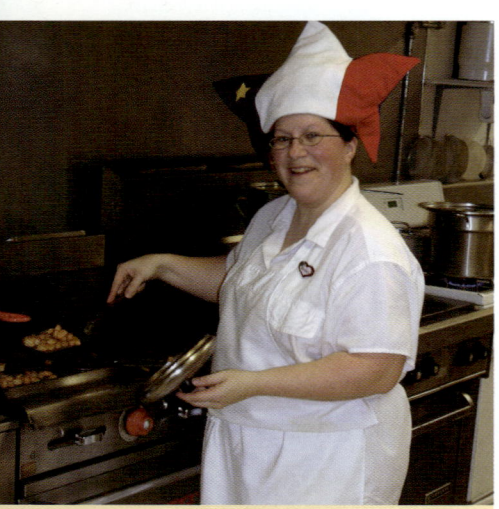

An Acadian chef prepares traditional Acadian meals for the large crowds drawn to Cheticamp for the Congrès. The resulting delicious food reflects Acadian traditions as much as her hat does!

asking questions, and scrutinizing the genealogical charts displayed around the large school gym.

The opening ceremonies were held at 9:45 a.m, and these were followed by two speakers: Chester Muise, who expounded on the history of the Mius family, and then Peter Crowell, archivist and historian at the Township Courthouse and Gaol in Tusket, who gave a brief but interesting account of the life of Benjamin Mius, who settled the area called "Les Ben" today. Both were very interesting and informative.

Dinner was served on site by La baie rapure, and though people had to wait in line for some time, there were no complaints. People were just happy to be there and build up an appetite for the Acadian dishes of rappie pie and fricot that awaited them. Hot dogs were served for those souls not brave enough to attempt the Acadian dishes.

The first part of the afternoon was spent doing what many had come to do—milling around and chatting. The photo display included old pictures of people and families from the Quinan and Amirault's Hill/ Surette's Island areas. It was heart-warming to watch and listen to people identifying with and rediscovering many of their folks ancestors represented in the photos. The genealogical charts in the gym were very popular as well, and were of great assistance to those searching for ancestors for their family trees.

At 3:30 p.m. the P'tit tyme began, the Dixacadie Dancers kicking off the party with a forty-five-minute routine illustrating the deportation of the Acadians. These young women, all between the ages of eight and twelve, put on an excellent performance that was much appreciated by all in attendance. They were a credit to *le peuple Acadien*. They were followed by local artists, who entertained until 5 p.m., when everyone was invited to make their way to the Island Fest, taking place on Surette's Island and lasting until the wee hours of the morning. Thus ended the Mius/ Muise/Meuse family reunion. The organizers were very pleased with the turnout, and grateful for the lovely weather and spirit of camaraderie that made this day one we will not soon forget.

MASS FOR THE DOUCET FAMILY REUNION, POINTE DE L'EGLISE, AUGUST 2, 2004

By Daniel Doucet

The God story is about remembering. Way back as far as Moses, the Jewish people were commanded to remember the Passover as the moment that defined them.

And in the spirit of Jesus, 400 years after our beginning as Acadians, some 250 years after we were scattered through the world by the Dispersion, we come together to remember and to find bits and pieces of ourselves.

We have all, each of us, become new people, married into different families, shared different cultures, attached ourselves to different lands, climates, politics, formed new alliances. As in fulfillment of the first reading, "Her branches will spread out, as beautiful as olive trees, fragrant as the forests of Lebanon."

This is the greater good, to become part of the greater human family. Jesus himself asked: "Who is my brother, my sister?" And the answer was not the Doucets or the Acadians,

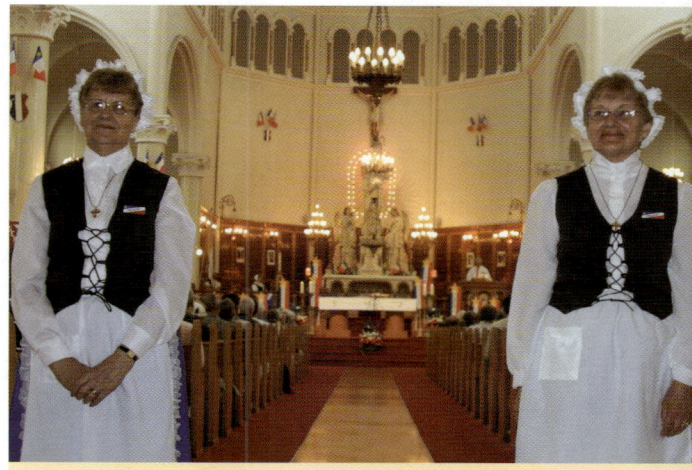

Acadian twin sisters Lucie Doucette Saulnier and Lucille Doucette Muise create a perfect pair for greeting the congregation at the Doucet family reunion mass at the beautiful Sainte-Marie Church, Church Point.

but "those who do the will of the Father." St. Paul said: "There is no Greek or Jew." We are all under the same God.

At the same time, while we are called upon to become world citizens, we become better world citizens and more spiritual people when we know ourselves better. And part of knowing ourselves, this group here today, is knowing our shared story as Acadians and more specifically, Doucets.

When my mother, a Chiasson, celebrated her ninetieth birthday five years ago, I decided that as a birthday gift, I would put together a book for her, based on stories my father told me on his deathbed, and on stories she had told me after he died. I included genealogies and old pictures. It was a lot of work, but it was fun. But what has been most amazing has been how the writing of this book has since precipitated an avalanche of new material and new people in my life. You might want to think twice before you do it. For example, I now have pictures of my great-grandfather Dominique Doucet's house, taken in 1905. The picture came to me from southern California. The cousin who visited me from California didn't even know what province the site of the house was in until he met me. An aunt had earlier given me a copy of Dominique's father's (Joe Doucet's) will, written in 1864. Another aunt gave me his cash box. He was born around 1800. That is only forty-five years after the Deportation. These links add flesh to our personal and family histories.

Even though it began as a tragedy, le Grand Dérangement has become a blessing to a family enriched by many experiences. The Doucets of Nova Scotia welcome those from away. We in turn look forward to visiting you in the new communities you have helped to create and to see what we have all done with the sparks of fire held by and passed on from our ancestors. Each spark of ourselves, of our shared past that we recover, can light new fires for us.

Some years ago, someone gave me two pictures of my great-grandfather, John à Basile Chiasson. I had never seen a picture of him before. But as a child, I had known his sons, my great-uncles. They seemed like giants to me, huge farmers, solid, old, and wise. I had imagined that, as their father, he would be bigger still and I would be much smaller. Instead, in the pictures, here was this tiny man, with wavy silver hair and a curled mustache, a ring on his little finger. He could have been a riverboat gambler. I was no longer dwarfed. I immediately felt a hundred times bigger. I fell in love with him and with a part of myself that I had never known.

We will all be made bigger by bits and pieces of ourselves that we discover here today and during the whole Congrès.

May you find many such pieces and may you fall in love with them and with yourself each time that you do.

What is called my character, or nature, is made up of infinite particles of inherited tendencies from my ancestors—those whose blood runs in my veins. A little seed of laziness comes from one grandparent and prodigality from the other one. One of them may been a moody person and a pessimist, while another was a jovial nature who always saw the sunny side of every event. One may have had a most satisfactory life as a philosopher; while another ambitious one never was content with actual conditions whatever they were. Some remote grandmother perhaps has stamped me with a fear of dogs and love of horses. There may be in me a bit of outlawry from some pirate forefather and dash of piety from one who was a saint.

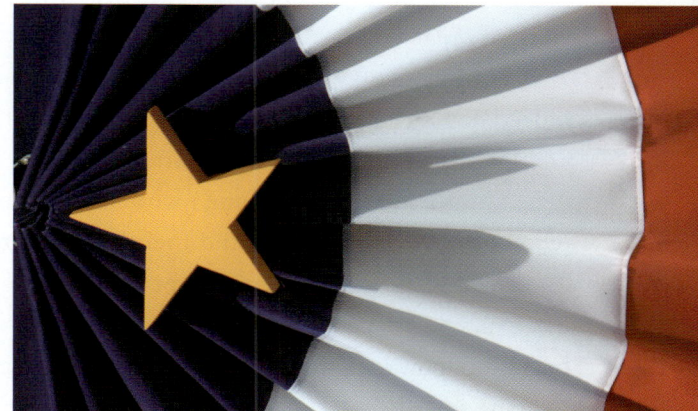

The brilliant colours of the Acadian flag are an enduring symbol of its proud heritage. The distinctive yellow star in the upper left corner represents Stella Maris, "the Star of the Sea," the patron saint of Acadians.

My so-called peculiarities: my gestures, my eyes and my mannerisms, I borrowed from all without exception. So everything passes on through my children. I am sewn between ancestry and posterity. I am a drop of water in a flowing river of time; a molecule in the mountain; a cell in a great family tree.

As we enter life we find all these fears and fancies; likes and dislikes, dispositions and temperament already made in the human beehive, and crawl into them so that they become a part of our true fibre, part of our personal texture, part of our frame and body.

This is our birthmark; this is our heritage.

– Oliver Wendell Holmes (1809–1894), Chief Justice, U.S. Supreme Court

This is the quote with which William Gerrior begins his book on the genealogy and history of the Gerrior, or Girouard, family. Monsieur Gerrior is a Nova Scotian school principal who has spent twenty-five years researching the various twists and turns in the Girouard family saga. He has traveled to Loudun and La Chaussée in the Loire valley of France, which is the original home region of many Acadian families, and he has walked the ground of his Gerrior ancestors. The book is full of stories, photographs, maps, and charts. In it, you can see the church where the Girouards and Aucoins celebrated their last mass in France before leaving for the New World. You can trace out the farms built along the rivers of Acadie where the Girouards settled—the Memramkouke in New Brunswick, the Dauphin River at Port-Royal, and then up to Grand-Pré, Pisiquid (Windsor), Cobequid (Truro), and Beaubassin (Amherst). William Gerroir's book is a work of great love.

It's people like William Gerrior who have saved the Acadian story from extinction—and it did indeed come close to extinction. In the 1950s, there was very little written about Acadian culture and history, and the old communities with their traditional lifestyles were disappearing. The elder generation, the men and women who had memories that went right back to the previous century, who knew with their heads and their hands more about Acadie than anyone, were beginning to leave us, and there were very few people who were paying much attention. The present always has a narcotic appeal, and the 1950s and 1960s were full of enchantments—new cars, radios, television, new kinds of jobs, new kinds of education, a bustling modern economy.

There was a very real danger that after more than three centuries, the Acadian people and their communities would disappear into modernity, losing not just their language but all connections with the past. I can remember my cousin Marcel Doucet being one of the only Acadian fiddlers in Cape Breton. I can remember when no one cared much for the old songs, or even if there was a French school in the village; when the news was always about how well someone was doing in some distant city; how quickly you could close the old farm up and sell off the contents to an antique dealer. But slowly, the Acadians pulled back from the edge of extinction, and the stories, songs, traditions, and family histories were saved by folklorists like Anselme Chiasson and Daniel Boudreau, musicians like Marcel Doucet and Edith Butler, writers like Antonine Maillet, family historians like William Gerroir and Pat Doucet Hayes, and education activists who realized that French language schools were essential.

A great deal has been accomplished, and the work still goes on at every level. I am astonished at how little I know and how much I learn at every family gathering. I came home from the Congrès with armloads of books, CDs, and memories of meeting new people, many of whom I am related to, albeit distantly. The Congrès itself has become a unique, perambulating institution, different from anything else on the planet—an event that emerges from the ground once every five years to help write a little more of the dynamic Acadian story.

Bonne fête, Acadie!

A group holding signs of different Acadians family names wait for the mass at Grand-Pré to begin. Catholicism is still linked with the Acadian culture, as historic Acadian life revolved around the parish: the church was the traditional meeting place for spiritual and community events.

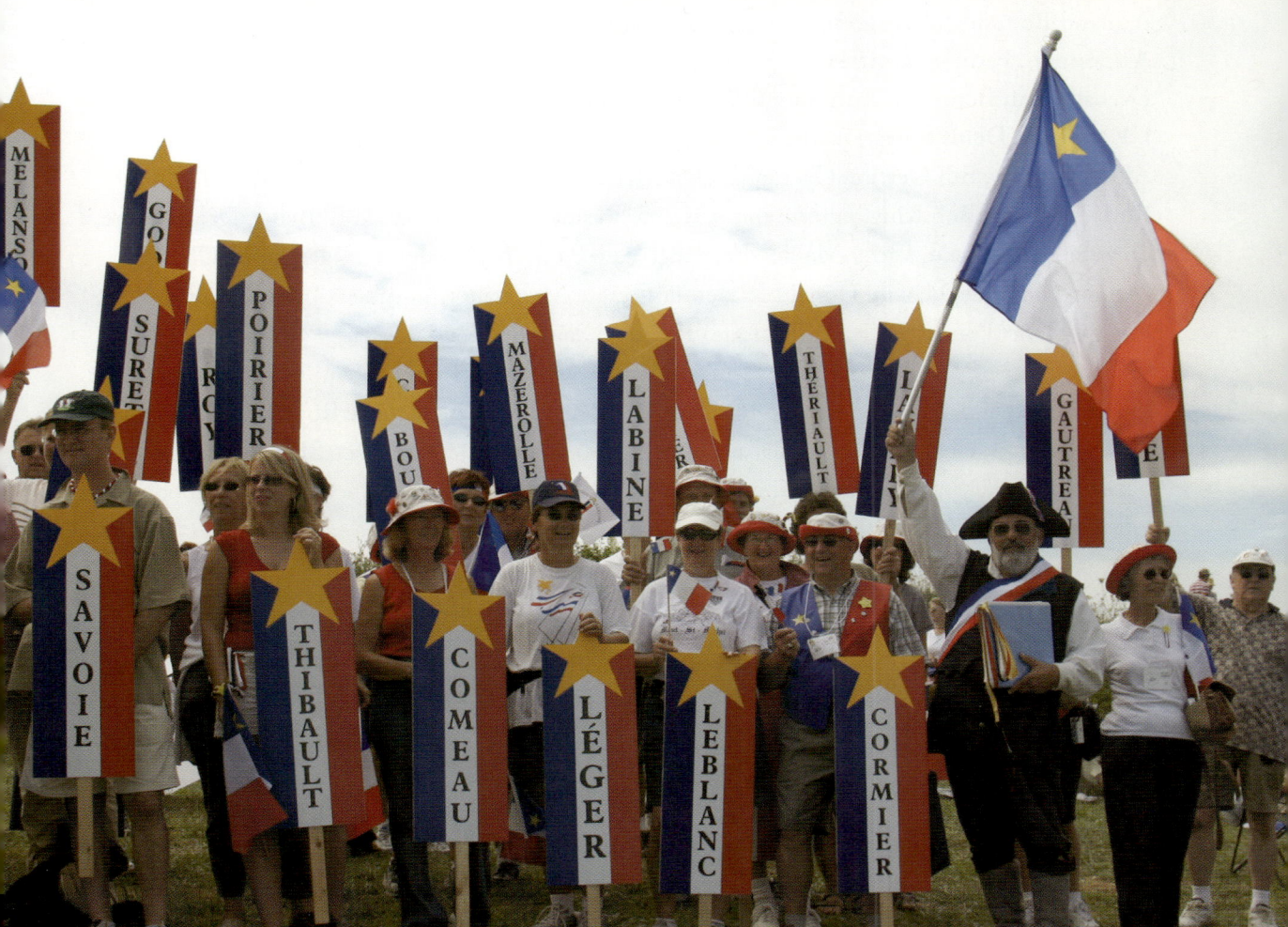

FAMILY REUNION ORGANIZERS

Alice Allain, Edouard Allain, Jean-Marie Allain, Pierre Arsenault, Jude Avery, Caroline Babin, Geneviève Babineau, Marc Bastarnache, Raoul Bastarnache, Claude Belliveau, Denise (Cordeau) Bennett, Lisa Berthier, Yves Blondin, Lloyd Boucher, Glenda Doucet Boudreau, Lis Bourgeois, Armand Bourque, Deanna Bourque, Kathy Bourque, Sheila Broussard, Geraldine Burke, Pierre A. Comeau, Franklin Cottreau, Anne Crossman, Ralph Daigle, Kenneth David, Evelyne Decoste, Jean Bernard d'Entremont, Paul Angus Desveaux, Emile Dugas, Daniel Dupuis, Larry J. Fitzgerald, Denis Forest, André Gaudet, Jeannette Gaudet, Vernon Gaudet, Raymond Gauvin, Albert Geddry, Bill Gerrior, Gaetan Godin, Martin Guidry, Gerald Hashey, Richard Hubbart, Ruth Hurlbert, Bob King, Janet Landry, Richard Landry, Marcel Daigle LeBlanc, Dara Légère, Theresa MacDonald, Vicky Maillet-LeBlanc, Jean-Pierre Mallet, Josette Marchand, Charlie Martin, Monique Martin, Donald Mazerolle, Teresa McEnaney, Yvonne Mosley, P. Earl Muise, Joseph-Henri Poirier, Barbara (Bourque) Pothier, Claire Pothier, Charlene Pothier, Michelle (Surette) Pottier, Ray Pottier, Tina Primeau, Françoise Prince, Theresa Rennie, Thelma Richard, Hugh Robichaud, Marie-Colombe Robichaud, Paulette Robichaud, Guy Roy, Yvon Samson, André Sandon, Charline (Thériault) Saulnier, Nadine Saulnier, Georges et Blanche Savoie, Irene Schofield, Duke Snyder, Gérard Thériault, Lynne Thériault, Richard Thibeau, René Thibodeau, Glenna (Thériault) Titus, Eric Trahan